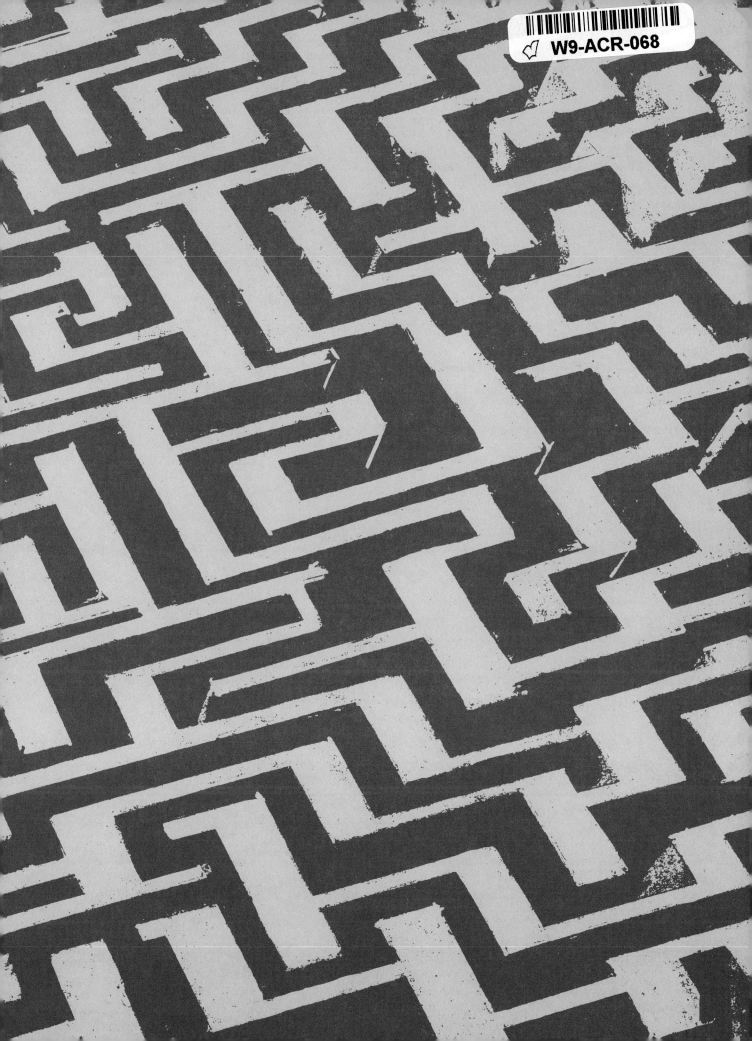

GHOSTS
AND
HAUNTINGS

QUEST FOR THE UNKNOWN

GHOSTS
AND
HAUNTINGS

Reader's
Digest

THE READER'S DIGEST ASSOCIATION, INC.
Pleasantville, New York/Montreal

Quest for the Unknown
Created, edited, and designed by DK Direct Limited

A DORLING KINDERSLEY BOOK

DK DIRECT LIMITED

Series Editor Richard Williams
Senior Editor Sue Leonard
Editors Kim Inglis, Tony Whitehorn
Editorial Research Julie Whitaker

Senior Art Editor Susie Breen
Designers Juliette Norsworthy, Alison Verity
Senior Picture Researcher Frances Vargo
Picture Researcher Lesley Coleman; **Picture Assistant** Sharon Southren

Editorial Director Jonathan Reed; **Design Director** Ed Day
Production Manager Ian Paton

Volume Consultant Hilary Evans
Commissioning Editor Peter Brookesmith
Contributors Loyd Auerbach, Hilary Evans, Melvin Harris,
Adam Hart-Davis, Peter Moss, Frank Smyth

Illustrators Roy Flooks, Gary Marsh, Peter Maynard, Jane Palmer,
Emma Parker, Steve Rawlings, Mike Shepherd
Photographers Simon Farnhell, Andrew Griffin,
Mark Hamilton, Steve Wallace, Alex Wilson

Library of Congress Cataloging in Publication Data

Ghosts and hauntings.
     p.   cm. — (Quest for the unknown)
    "A Dorling Kindersley book" — T.p. verso.
    Includes index.
    ISBN 0-89577-493-3
    1. Ghosts. 2. Haunted houses.   3. Apparitions. I. Reader's
Digest Association. II. Series.
BF1461.G49 1993
133.1—dc20   91-39630

Printed in the United States of America

FOREWORD

*S*TORIES OF GHOST SIGHTINGS have been told in every culture since time began. Some such accounts have described earthbound spirits, while others have reported what are known as crisis apparitions, in which a dying person appears to a loved one at the moment of death. And still others have told of ghosts of animals. There have even been tales of ghosts of inanimate objects, such as trains, coaches, and ships — and such stories continue today.

People have long speculated on the causes of such phenomena. Yet it was not until the mid-19th century that ghost sightings were actually scientifically investigated. For the Society for Psychical Research in London, and later its American counterpart, were founded with the specific purpose of finding out whether ghosts existed or not. Over the years since then, investigators into the paranormal, "ghostbusters," psychics, mediums, and a host of scientists, doctors, and other types of researchers have gathered an impressive wealth of information on the subject.

In this volume, we discuss various ghost experiences, and present the arguments for and against the validity of such cases. We examine firsthand accounts, often backed up by independent witnesses, and present the facts with an open mind. We look at the methods that investigators employ in ghost detection, and discuss the numerous hypotheses put forward by the experts in the field. However, despite numerous theories, accounts, investigations, and first-person reports, the quest for the truth continues. The question: "Do ghosts exist?" is one that may never be answered.

— The Editors

CONTENTS

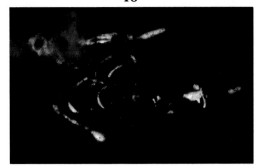

A HAUNTING EXPERIENCE

Many people claim to have seen ghosts. And such phantoms have taken various forms, some ghoulish and terrifying, some mischievous, and some mundane. What follows is an account of an alleged modern-day haunting, by the California ghost-hunter Loyd Auerbach.

❝ It was a fairly normal day in 1985 at my office at John F. Kennedy University in Orinda, California. I was following up a number of interview possibilities, as well as handling requests for information about parapsychology in general and ghosts in particular. At the time the comedy movie *Ghostbusters* (1984) was a smash hit, and I had recently been tagged a 'real-life ghostbuster' by the media.

"The telephone rang, and I picked it up. 'Mr. Auerbach,' a female voice said, 'you

may not believe this, but we have a ghost in our house.' The caller, Jean, was an attorney living in Livermore, an old community east of Orinda. The family had moved into an old house about three years before, and apparently Jean, her husband, Steve, and her mother felt something unusual, though warm and inviting, about the house from the first time they visited it.

"After a few months, Jean and Steve began catching glimpses of a female figure moving through the house. While the apparition appeared to them on more than one occasion, they never spoke about the figure to each other, until their 12-year-old son, Alan, began talking about her. It was after the revelation that Alan could see and even communicate with the ghostly figure that Jean's mother, Mary, confessed that she had seen the apparition several times.

Secret information

"I leaned back in my chair as Jean's story unfolded, my interest growing with each bit of information she passed on.

"It wasn't as simple as Alan saying 'Hey Mom, have you been seeing a ghost around here?' she told me. Alan came to her with questions about the house and its previous owner. He also made comments about things he said he 'knew' had gone on in the past in the house and in the area around it.

Inexplicable knowledge

"For example, there was a doll collection they had bought in the estate sale. Alan told Jean stories about several of the dolls and when they were purchased. It was as if someone else had told him. He asked Jean about pieces of furniture and whether she thought they might have been brought into the house at specific times. He commented in a knowing way on parties that had gone on in the house. In addition, his description of the prior owner: what she looked like, how she worked outside around the house on plants, and her other habits, were

confirmed by the neighbors (who claimed that they had never talked to Alan about her).

"As to the neighborhood, Alan asked about the years that certain houses had been built in the area, and described some of the inhabitants of those houses years before. Once her curiosity was piqued, Jean learned from neighbors and local records that various things Alan had told her were absolutely correct. They had happened, yet there was no apparent source for Alan's knowledge.

Earlier occupant

"Finally, Jean asked her son directly how he knew so much. Alan's response was: 'Lois told me.' Lois was the previous owner of the house, who died in 1980.

"Alan had apparently been seeing and conversing with Lois for over a year, often on a daily basis. He never told his parents about it because, he said, Lois didn't feel it was appropriate. After Alan revealed his discourses with the spirit, Steve and Jean's mother admitted that they, too, had seen the ghost (though Lois never spoke to them).

"So why was she calling in a 'ghost-buster?' I wondered aloud.

"As with a number of cases of apparitional encounters, Jean and her family were curious but a bit concerned. They were curious about Lois herself and her apparent existence as a disembodied entity. They were concerned that Alan would grow up to be a normal teen.

"'Have you thought about taking him to a counselor? I can recommend a couple who won't laugh him off as crazy because he's seeing a ghost,' I suggested.

"Jean was way ahead of me, since she had already taken Alan for a couple of sessions with a psychotherapist. Not because she thought there was anything wrong with him, but because she wanted to make sure the contacts with Lois would leave Alan without any negative impact or influence. The counselor was willing to speak with me, since he, too, found the whole case interesting.

"There was a doll collection they had bought in the estate sale. Alan told Jean stories about several of the dolls and when they were purchased. It was as if someone else had told him."

11

"'Can you come out and check on the ghost?' Jean finally asked.

"'Let me meet with the counselor first, so I have all the information from him, then I'll make it out to see you.'

"She agreed heartily, then added, 'Oh, and Alan wanted me to make sure that you had no blasters or devices to get rid of Lois. Alan and Lois saw television commercials for *Ghostbusters*, and, apparently, she was just concerned that you were going to blast her out of the walls. What equipment do you use?'

Average accessories

"I assured Jean that the proton packs and particle accelerators they had seen were the stuff of motion pictures. 'In fact people are generally disappointed by our lack of high-tech equipment. Tell Alan and Lois not to worry about it. I'll be armed with a camera and a tape recorder and that's all.'

"A few days later, I found myself sitting in a pizza place waiting for Alan's counselor to show up. Soon a casually dressed man in his mid-thirties appeared and introduced himself as Bill.

"Over lunch, we discussed ideas about psychic phenomena and apparitions and hauntings in particular. Although Bill was not knowledgeable in my field, I found him to be interested and open-minded. Unlike any number of psychotherapists, he was willing to take into account subjective experiences without the need to have proof of their objectivity. In other words, whether Bill believed in ghosts or not, he was sure that Alan and his family did. Leaving that belief where it was, Bill worked with Alan to see if he was otherwise well adjusted. He was.

"Several days later, I headed for Livermore. With me were Joanna and Kip, who were going to help me with the interviews and investigation. During the drive, I started the tape recorder to get their initial input as I repeated what I knew about the case so far. Both decided it sounded interesting, and the

conversation turned to other things. Little did we realize how significant this casual discussion would turn out to be later in our investigation.

"Kip, who worked at the university as well, was a student in the transpersonal counseling program. During our conversation, we learned that Kip had been a professional dancer for a number of years. I had known Kip for a while and had heard nothing of this before.

"Joanna, to whom I was married at the time, began talking about her job, how she didn't like it, and the kind of job she was looking for.

"My own part of the conversation was a bit mundane. The car had been acting up and I was hoping to get a new one soon after. When Kip asked what kind of car I wanted, Joanna and I talked about a particular couple we had both liked, down to the colors.

"Shortly after, we arrived at the house. Livermore itself is an old (for northern California) community in the Livermore Valley, a wine-producing area with one of the oldest wineries in California. The house had been built in the early 1900's.

Antique accommodation

"As we entered, we saw dark woods and antiques. The house was in excellent condition, and apparently some of the furniture and fixtures were original.

"Since Alan had revealed his contact with Lois, the family had compared notes and learned that they had all seen Lois more than once.

"We questioned all three on the approximate dates of the events. Their answers told us that Lois was fairly prolific in her appearances, even though Alan was the only one she visited on a daily basis and the only one able to hear her speak. Throughout the interview I got the

impression Alan was listening to more voices than I could hear.

"I finally asked him if Lois was there as well.

"He nodded, so I asked where she was. He smiled and suggested we try to figure it out.

"Unfortunately, as with most investigators in my field, I have little psychic ability of my own and have yet to see a ghost. I let the subject drop for the moment and suggested that we take a walk around the house.

The full picture

"They all added to the tour with commentary on their experiences in each of the rooms. Alan related bits of history about Lois and her lifetime in the house. Given that there were many items in the house from that lifetime, one could almost imagine her there.

"As we walked around the outside of the house, we began to get a fuller picture of its previous owner.

"Lois lived in the house from birth to death. She was from a family with history in the area, a family not without means. She was a bit of a socialite, people taking the long trip from San Francisco to visit and come to her parties. Her death in 1980 was of natural causes after a long and apparently fulfilled life.

"There was quite a bit more, most of it anecdotes and family stories from Lois's lifetime that she had apparently passed on to Alan. Most of it was un-verifiable, as with most anecdotes told without physical evidence. But Jean set out to track down an elderly gentleman who was Lois's only living relative. Jean, as

> "I got the impression Alan was listening to more voices than I could hear. I finally asked him if Lois was there as well. He nodded, so I asked where she was. He smiled and suggested we try to figure it out."

"To Alan, Lois generally looked like an elderly woman. Sometimes, however, she appeared as a girl his own age, or a girl about 6 years old, sometimes around 20, and at other times in middle age."

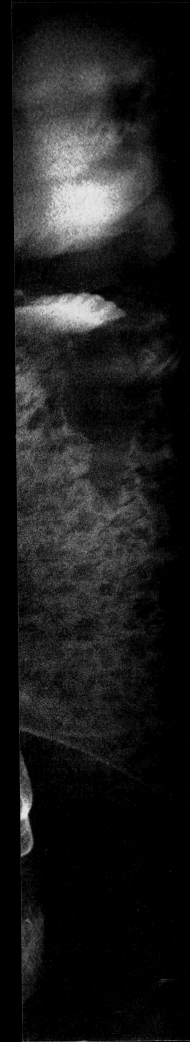

an attorney who had much of her practice in family law, had utilized the services of private investigators in the past to track down missing spouses or 'stolen' children. Through the help of one of them, she succeeded in finding this cousin. When he was told some of Alan's stories, he was quite surprised, since he had witnessed a number of events in them and knew about others. But he was confused as to how anyone could have any knowledge of them, since they hadn't been recorded in any fashion, and Lois had left no diaries.

Accurate details

"As we sat down again in the living room, having marveled at the detailed information Alan had passed along to his mother, he told us a bit more about Lois and what she looked like to him.

"Lois, he said, would show up daily, though never at inconvenient times. She often popped in to tell Alan stories about her life and family, or just to watch TV with him (which is how she saw commercials for *Ghostbusters*). To Alan, Lois generally looked like an elderly woman. Sometimes, however, she appeared as a girl his own age, or a girl about 6 years old, sometimes around 20, and at other times in middle age.

"'Why do you think that is?' I asked.

"He said he knew for sure why that was, since she had told him. 'That's how she felt that day.' In other words, if she felt six years old on a given day, that was how Alan saw her.

"When I asked again if Lois was with us, he pointed at the empty easy chair in the corner. 'Her favorite chair,' he said.

"We proceeded with the interview, though we often addressed questions to the empty chair where Alan claimed the ghost sat. Alan was acting as the 'translator' for a ghost who could hear us but whom we couldn't hear or understand. I had the feeling there really was someone in that chair.

"'Did her clothes change or did she wear the same thing every day?' I asked.

"Alan said that her clothes, like her age, seemed to change, based on how she felt on a given day. Mary and Jean said that the apparition they had seen wore different clothing for each sighting.

"The situation provided me with the unique opportunity of being able to ask an alleged ghost a few burning questions. According to Lois (as told to us by Alan), spirits are without form and substance, a free-floating consciousness with no physical means to communicate or even be seen. All spirit communication occurs through telepathy, through mind-to-mind communication.

"How she is 'seen' is through a similar process, as her own mind projects an image into the mind of the witness. Why she is seen a certain way or wearing certain clothes on a given day is based more on her own internal image of herself than any sort of 'astral body.' And because the 'image' of her was only a mental projection, I had to forget trying to photograph her.

Unique cross-examination

"As to why Alan could make contact with her but others couldn't, Lois answered that she felt at ease with Alan and that he must have been more psychic than the rest of the family. So she made a real effort to communicate with him.

"The conversation continued this way for a bit. To me, it was beyond belief that a 12-year-old boy could somehow fake all this knowledge, especially since what he was saying was rarely written up in books about ghosts (at that time).

"Joanna and Kip then turned the conversation to another topic. 'Why was Lois still there?' they wondered.

"Again, Lois surprised us. She wasn't sure *how* she could still be around, but she knew several other things. She loved her home and she really liked the new family in it. That was fine, but then came the 'kicker.'

"Apparently, since she had been such a socialite during life, and never an avid churchgoer, she was nervous about

where she'd 'end up...heaven or hell.' Since she felt she could stay in her house, and she wasn't sure what her spiritual destination was, or even whether there really was a heaven and a hell, she figured: 'Why take the chance?' So she stayed in her lifetime home.

"While we were trying to take that in, I asked if Lois had any questions for us.

Reciprocal inquiries
"Alan looked over at the empty chair and nodded. 'She has one question for each of you.'

"She asked Kip, 'How long were you a professional dancer?'

"She then asked Joanna why she was so unhappy in her job and when she was going to start looking for another.

"Finally, she asked me about the car I was considering getting, specifically about the color and model and what was wrong with the car I had.

"I realized immediately that all three questions related to the private conversation the three of us had had on the drive to Livermore. I was sure that we had not discussed those topics since setting foot in the house (the content of the tape later confirmed this). In addition, since the tape with the car conversation on it was in my recorder for a good part of the session, then in my pocket, there was no way that Alan could have listened to it, especially since he was with us throughout our visit.

"I asked how Lois knew to ask those questions. Alan looked at Lois's chair, then sheepishly answered: 'She hitched a ride with you on your drive here and eavesdropped.' Apparently, Lois was not convinced about our benign intentions and wanted to make sure we weren't bringing any strange 'ghostbusting' equipment with us.

"This final exchange really drove home that we were either dealing with a *very* psychic youngster, or a ghost. And we thought that the spirit hypothesis seemed to fit all points much better. A ghost was the more likely explanation.

"On that last note, Lois apparently took her leave, as did we. Alan was a well-adjusted boy with a friendly ghost. There was little to be concerned with from a parapsychological standpoint.

"Every once in a while I spoke with Jean. Lois is, to this day, still in that house in Livermore, although she appeared less and less even to Alan as he grew up and discovered 'real girls.'

Traveling light
"Of course, there is one issue still left unresolved that I really should have asked Lois about.

"Can ghosts just 'fly' or 'teleport' from one place to another, wherever they want to go? Or are ghosts limited by our standard means of travel, like the apparition the actor Patrick Swayze portrayed in the film *Ghost* (1990)? (He had to take the subway, like every other New Yorker.)

"If Lois really 'hitched a ride' in my car on our drive to Livermore, just how did she get to the car in the first place? **"**

Loyd Auerbach
August 1992

COMMENT
Loyd Auerbach approaches his chosen profession of ghost-hunting in a methodical, apparently unbiased way. And yet we must assume that having set himself up as a ghost-hunter, he believes in the existence of ghosts — even though he admits he has never seen one himself. This case yielded interesting information that helps to shape some ideas of what ghosts might be. But the investigation is purely subjective and produced no physical "proof" of a ghostly presence in the house. So, although Auerbach's modern attitude is far removed from the irrational investigations of earlier times, he comes no closer to proving the existence of ghosts than his flamboyant antecedents. However, there is no disputing the fact that Lois's ghost was very real to the family living in her home.

> "I asked how Lois knew to ask those questions. Alan looked at Lois's chair, then sheepishly answered: 'She hitched a ride with you on your drive here and eavesdropped.'"

CHAPTER ONE

SPECTERS AND PHANTOMS

Ghost stories have appeared throughout the history of humankind. They have been recounted in all cultures, and in many countries. Indeed, they continue to be reported today. But is there such a thing as a typical ghost story?

In the letters of the Roman historian, Pliny the Younger (A.D. 62–113), there is a document addressed to a colleague, Licinius Sura, that contains what many would consider a typical ghost story. In Athens, during the first century of the Christian era, strange noises like the clanging of iron were heard from a certain house. When first detected, the sounds seemed a long way off, but gradually they grew louder. The occupants claimed that an old man then appeared — thin and squalid in appearance, with a long beard and bristling hair, and with shackles on his hands and legs. This apparition so terrified the onlookers that they became ill and eventually decided to leave the house.

At about that time, it happened that a philosopher named Athenodorus was looking for accommodation. He saw the notice board outside the house and so inquired about the property. He was surprised at the low price being asked, but believing he had found a bargain, he signed a contract, and moved in.

Rattled its chains
Athenodorous planned to spend his first night writing, but when it grew dark, he

Scholarly debate
The Roman historian Pliny the Younger was one among many who considered that the question of ghosts merited detailed and thorough debate.

was disturbed by the same sounds as had driven away the former occupants. The sounds grew much louder until it seemed to him that they must be in the same room; he claimed that when he looked up he saw a phantom beckoning to him. Athenodorus indicated that he intended to continue with his writing, but the phantom rattled its chains and beckoned a second time.

More curious than alarmed, the practical philosopher took up his lamp and accompanied the figure, which turned and led him out of the room into the courtyard of the house, where it abruptly vanished. However, Athenodorus noted the spot where the specter had disappeared and marked it with some leaves before returning inside to resume his work.

Practical solution
The next day, so the story goes, Athenodorus went to the city magistrates and suggested that the ground should be dug up in the area where the ghost had disappeared. They agreed, and men were sent to carry out the task, whereupon a pile of bones was found, surrounded by chains. These were gathered up and given a proper burial. From that time on the haunting ceased.

This ancient ghost story is simple enough, yet it contains what many would consider the essential elements of a ghostly tale — mysterious sounds; a figure that seems to appear from the dead; a mysterious message; and a satisfactory conclusion that apparently explains all and resolves all.

Simple stories
Most ghost stories are simple in outline, and often the simpler they are, the more impressive they appear. They have been recounted since time immemorial — indeed they form a continuous thread that crosses cultural and physical boundaries. An ancient Egyptian, a medieval monk, a Renaissance scholar, and an Australian aborigine, for example, might not have had a great deal in

> **A pile of bones was found, surrounded by chains. These were gathered up and given a proper burial....the haunting ceased.**

common, but one thing they all shared was a tradition of ghost stories. This tradition continues today. What follows, for example, is a contemporary tale collected by Canadian author John Robert Colombo and related in his book *Extraordinary Experiences* (1989).

Mrs. Lois Mulhall who lived in Bridge-water, Nova Scotia, at the time, related the following story: "It was during Schooner Week in Nova Scotia. That's when all the schooners from Nova Scotia and the U.S. get together for races. My son, an airforce pilot, and his wife were home visiting. In the house were those two, my husband, myself, a friend from Toronto, my daughter, a stepson, another son, and who knows who else? But here's what happened.

"By mid-week, we were all exhausted from racing and partying, so we went to bed early. It was a very quiet night, foggy, no wind. Our bedroom had a very thick shag area-carpet on the floor and we had to drag the door across it with force when we wanted to close it. The door was wide open, well past the area-carpet. Near the door there was a mobile of abalone shells that tinkled when there was a breeze."

Mrs. Mulhall said that after everyone had fallen asleep in the big old remodeled farmhouse, she was suddenly awakened by the sound of her bedroom door slamming shut. She claimed that she heard the doorknob rattle and thought someone wanted to talk to her: "I was too exhausted — people always bring me their problems — so I woke my husband, saying, 'Someone's trying to open the bedroom door!'"

Slamming door

Mr. Mulhall asked how the door had closed and his wife told him that she had heard it slam shut, adding that the knob must have turned and locked itself. Even though this seemed unlikely, her husband got up to investigate. Mrs. Mulhall claimed that she then rolled over and tried to go back to sleep, but she remembered just before she dropped off to sleep, hearing her husband walk across the room, open the door, and then come back to bed, saying, "You won't believe what happened to me."

> **He saw a woman coming toward him. She was tall and slender....He could not see her feet, but she seemed to be gliding across the floor.**

Mrs. Mulhall continued: "Next morning I rose at five o'clock because I had to feed the gang and we had to pack lunches. While enjoying my first cup of coffee, Ria, my friend from Toronto, came into the kitchen and said, 'You won't believe what happened to me last night.' Well, I'm not really a sociable person before coffee and really wasn't listening to her. Then my husband, Les, entered the kitchen. Ria said to him, 'Les, you'll never believe what happened to me last night.' He interrupted: 'It can never top what happened to me!'

Mr. Mulhall said that when his wife had awakened him the previous night, and he had gone to investigate the disturbance, he was surprised to hear the abalone shells tinkling, even though there was no wind. He realized that

somehow the door had slammed shut, and when he walked across the floor to open it, he claimed he saw a woman coming toward him. He described her as tall and slender, wearing a white nightgown with a tie around the waist. She had one arm raised, as though she was touching her hair. Her other arm hung down at her side. He could not see her feet, but he thought that she seemed to be gliding across the floor.

Spectral sleepwalker

Mrs. Mulhall again took up the story: "My husband said he thought the woman was Cheryl, my son's wife, and that she was sleepwalking. Not knowing what else to do (you know the old thing about not waking up sleepwalkers), he was going to turn her round and guide her back to the third floor where she and my son Peter were sleeping. But

Journey of the soul
The ancient Egyptians believed that after death the soul began a journey into an afterlife. This funerary papyrus depicts the weighing of the soul. The god of the dead weighs the deceased's heart. If it proves laden with sin the soul will be doomed to wander in the underworld as a spirit.

Aboriginal art
Australian aborigines believe that each individual is reincarnated at birth and returns to his original spirit state at death. Cave paintings of spirit figures such as these indicate that, as in other cultures, the aborigines had their own ghost stories to tell.

Tragic sighting
Lois Mulhall's son Peter and his wife Cheryl. It is claimed that their apparitions were seen nine days before they were killed in a plane crash.

when he reached out to turn her around, he walked right through her. Thinking he was hallucinating from too much 'ocean time,' he went and opened the door and found that there was nobody there. Then he came back to the bed and said: 'You won't believe what happened to me!'"

Half a ghost?

Mr. Mulhall's account was greeted with incredulity, and then Ria began hers. She had been allocated the bedroom next to that of Mr. and Mrs. Mulhall, and she said she was awakened by the loud slam of their door. Even though her door was closed, she said she saw someone standing just inside the door. She

Spirit mask
In all cultures, the tradition of ghosts and spirits plays an important role. This barkcloth mask from Papua New Guinea represents a spirit, and is worn on ceremonial occasions.

described the figure as a tall young man. She believed him to be Mrs. Mulhall's son Peter. Then she allegedly noticed that only half of him appeared to be standing in the doorway and the door was closed. She thought she was hallucinating, so she sat up and moved sideways for another perspective. But apparently he was still there, or at least half of him.

The strangest part of this ghost story is that both Mr. Mulhall and Ria identified the people they saw, tentatively, as Cheryl and Peter. Nine days later Peter and Cheryl were killed in an accident in a light aircraft on their way back to the air force base at Chatham, New Brunswick, where Peter was stationed.

Ghostly tradition

Neither of these incidents — the story related by Athenodorus or its modern Canadian counterpart — is particularly dramatic, except to those who were involved with them. As ghost stories go, they are fairly commonplace. What is interesting, however, is that such stories have been told since earliest times (Pliny's tale is by no means the oldest ghost story in existence) and that they are still being told.

What exactly is a ghost story? It is an account of an experience in which the narrator reportedly saw someone or something that looked like a real, living person — but which was not. So how does the narrator know that the thing wasn't alive? Sometimes the observer

> **She thought she was hallucinating, so she moved sideways for another perspective. But apparently he was still there, or at least half of him.**

may have recognized the seeming presence as someone known to be dead or known to be a thousand miles away at the time. Sometimes the figure's behavior may have alerted the witness to conclude that it was not real — it may have suddenly appeared in the room, or vanished, or walked through walls. It may have been transparent, or when the witness tried to approach or touch it, it may have proved insubstantial.

But that does not conclusively prove that it exists or does not exist. Although sometimes more than one person will claim to see a figure, frequently animals appear to react to it, and occasionally, though very rarely, a camera may record something resembling it.

In search of an explanation

When Pliny the Younger recounted the story of Athenodorus, he stated that such stories merit prolonged and profound consideration. Many individuals through the following centuries have shared that opinion: historians, psychic investigators, "ghostbusters," and psychologists, to name a few, have attempted to explain or interpret such stories. Yet despite all their efforts, the ghost phenomenon remains a baffling enigma.

Skeptics declare that the evidence accumulated from numerous reported ghost sightings, despite its quantity, is lacking in quality; that is to say, there is no positive proof that any of these incidents occur as recounted, and that they may easily be attributed to chance or coincidence, hoax or rumor, imagination or illusion.

The ghost experience

Despite the fact that some people continue to report experiences that seem remarkable to them, scientists have refused to concede that anything remarkable is actually taking place. The shortcoming of this skeptical attitude, some feel, is a failure to distinguish between the ghost itself, and the ghost experience. Yet, from the time of the very first ghost stories, there was often a practical aspect to the ghost experience. Even though the ghost could be deemed insubstantial, its manifestation had substantial consequences. This is illustrated in the case of Athenodorus by the discovery of the bones.

There are thousands of recorded instances where the seeing of a ghost has led to practical results of one kind or another: we shall look at several such cases during the course of this

book. To attribute them all to chance or coincidence, some feel, would be a mistake. And yet it is possible to understand the dilemma of skeptics. Ghosts seem to happen so rarely, so ambiguously, and so elusively, that it is hard to find a place for them in the real world of everyday experience. In our daily lives, we make a clear distinction between things that are real — people, places, things we can see, feel, smell, hear, and touch — and things that are unreal — dreams, fantasies, fictions, thoughts. There are few other things that, like the ghost, manage somehow to combine these two crucial elements — the real and the unreal.

Photographic evidence?
It is rare for a ghost to be captured on film. This photograph allegedly shows the apparition of Lord Combermere, of Combermere Abbey in Cheshire, England, in his library. The photograph was taken by Sybell Corbet at about 2 P.M. on December 5, 1891 — at about the same time Lord Combermere was being buried in Wrenbury, four miles away.

Ghost guard
In many primitive societies, the line between the human and the spirit world is judged to be a fine one. In the Nicobar Islands, in the Bay of Bengal, images such as this one were placed in houses to protect inhabitants from the intrusion of otherworldly entities.

"They came from tombs in mummy bandages with cheeks of decaying flesh, flat noses, and eyes of horror."

VITAL WITNESS

Because ghosts have an uncertain status in the scheme of things, attitudes toward them are inconsistent. Yet how they are perceived may be influenced by the creed or culture of the witness.

*I*N ANCIENT EGYPT, where ghost stories were plentiful, ghosts were objects of dread, as folklorist Donald Mackenzie explains in his book *Egyptian Myth and Legend* (1913): "The Egyptian ghosts, the enemies of the living, were of repulsive aspect. They came from tombs in mummy bandages with cheeks of decaying flesh, flat noses, and eyes of horror, and entered a room with averted faces, which were suddenly turned on children, who at once died of fright. They killed sleeping babes by sucking their breath when they kissed, or rather smelled, them, and if children were found crying they rocked them to sleep — the sleep of death."

Why were ancient Egyptian ghosts different from ghosts anywhere else? Were they a species on their own? Of course not. It is clear from Mackenzie's account that this view of ghosts was based not on objective fact but on fears and expectations — ancient Egyptians experienced what they expected to experience; they saw what the priests had taught them they would see.

Cultural differences

Throughout the greater part of human history, the beliefs of the ordinary, everyday person, at least in part, have been dictated by authority figures, such as priests or shamans, who interpret experience in the light of their own particular belief systems. So if, for instance, the priests of a certain culture conclude that ghosts are evil spirits, their people, in turn, will most likely view ghosts in that form. And in different cultures and communities throughout history, each society has seen the kind of ghost it expects to see. Brought up to believe that ghosts are horrid and harmful, people will see horrid and harmful ghosts; in a different climate of belief, they will regard ghosts differently.

Ghosts of the mind

The tendency of many ghost stories to reflect the prevailing belief-system encourages skeptics to say that they must then be a purely psychological phenomenon — that ghostly images are obviously generated by the mind. Consequently, this line of reasoning goes, ghosts as such are not to be taken seriously. Up

Mummified corpse
Because the ancient Egyptian dead were mummified, Egyptians expected to see their ghosts swathed in bandages.

to a point this might be valid. Clearly, in a very real sense, people do indeed see what their minds are conditioned to see.

It is important, therefore, to recognize that the ghost experience is made up of two elements: the phenomenon itself, whatever it may be, and the way the witness responds to that phenomenon. This second item is an obstacle to understanding the first, because when someone tells a ghost story, the listener inevitably hears it in the witness's own terms, which are apt to be affected by his or her cultural background and other elements as well. In evaluating any ghost story, therefore, the circumstances in which it is told must be taken into account. The person telling the story, and their previous experiences, should be evaluated, along with the prevailing cultural and religious climate in which that person lives.

Biased storyteller?

This approach may be applied to a specific story: In July 1895 Capt. Joshua Slocum, the great American sailor, had a remarkable experience during the course of his historic solo voyage around the world in his ship the *Spray*. The story is recorded in Slocum's book *Sailing Alone Around the World* (1900). Slocum was sailing in the Atlantic, between the Azores and Gibraltar, when he ran into very bad, squally weather. At the same time he was afflicted with severe stomach cramps and, without taking in his sails as he knew he should do in such bad weather, he went below and threw himself on the floor of the boat's cabin, in considerable distress and great pain.

The Spray
In 1895, in this tiny 37-foot vessel, Joshua Slocum became the first person to sail around the world single-handed. Fourteen years later Slocum set off in the same ship from Bristol, Rhode Island, headed for the Orinoco River in South America. Tragically, he and the Spray were never seen again.

Capt. Joshua Slocum

Slocum did not know how long he lay in the cabin, as he was delirious, but when he came to he realized that his ship was being engulfed by heavy seas. He looked up toward the deck, and surprisingly he saw a man at the helm. "His rigid hand, grasping the spokes of the wheel, held them as in a vice," he wrote. "One may imagine my astonishment. His rig was that of a foreign sailor, and the large red cap he wore was cock-billed over his left ear, and all was set off with shaggy black whiskers.

Ghostly guidance

"He would have been taken for a pirate in any part of the world. While I gazed upon his threatening aspect I forgot the storm, and wondered if he had come to cut my throat. This he seemed to divine. 'Señor,' said he, doffing his cap, 'I have come to do you no harm.'

"And a smile, the faintest in the world, but still a smile, played on his face, which seemed not unkind when he spoke. 'I am one of Columbus' crew, the pilot of the *Pinta*, come to aid you. Lie quiet, señor captain, and I will guide your ship tonight. You have a calentura [a reference to the debilitating stomach cramps] but you will be all right tomorrow....You did wrong to mix cheese with plums....' I thought what a very devil he was to carry sail. Again, as if he read my mind, he exclaimed, 'Yonder is the *Pinta* ahead, we must overtake her. Give her sail, give her sail!'"

Adventurous phantom

Next day Slocum found that the *Spray* was still heading as he had left her — "Columbus himself could not have held her more exactly on her course. I felt grateful to the old pilot, but I marvelled some that he had not taken in the jib. I was getting much better now, but was very weak...I fell asleep. Then who should visit me but my old friend of the night before, this time, of course, in a dream. 'You did well last night to take my advice,' said he, 'and if you would, I

▶ PAGE 28

PERMISSION TO RETURN

In the past some religious believers asserted that it was possible for the spirits of the dead to return to earth as ghosts — while others adamantly rejected the concept.

IN THE 16TH AND 17TH CENTURIES many Roman Catholics believed that souls in purgatory could obtain permission to revisit earth, while Protestants denied this possibility. This led to fierce controversy as to the nature of ghosts, with some Catholics seeing them as returning spirits of the deceased, and many Protestants considering them to be diabolic impostors.

When the Swiss Protestant priest Louis Lavater wrote *Of Ghostes and Spirites Walking by Nyght* in 1572, he was making an all-out attack on the reality of ghosts. He starts by showing how easy it is to mistake or misinterpret natural things for ghosts, then he accuses Catholic priests and monks

> ## "The Diuell... for the moste part is the worker of these things," for he "can chaunge himselfe into all shapes and fashions."
>
> **Louis Lavater**

of encouraging the notion of ghosts to inspire fear and reverence among the common people. However, he does not deny the ghost experience altogether: "No man can deny, but that many honest & credible persons of both kinds, aswel men as women, of whom som ar living, & some alredy departed, which haue & do affirm that they haue...seen & hard spirits." But, says Lavater, these spirits are not what they seem. Rather, it is "the Diuell, who for the moste part is the worker of these things,"

for he "can chaunge himselfe into all shapes and fashions." Response came in the form of a treatise, *Discourse on Spectres, Visions and Apparitions of Spirits* by the French lawyer Pierre Le Loyer. He agrees with Lavater that many ghosts are misinterpretations and deceptions, but states that there are many cases that cannot be dismissed in this way. He is even ready to admit that many are indeed the work of the devil. But he insists that those cases which purport to be spirits returning from purgatory are precisely what they claim to be, spirits of the dead who are permitted by God to come back in order to right some wrong or to obtain help from the living.

The devil's work?

Such arguments would attract little notice and few dedicated supporters today: Not many people nowadays would consider it likely that ghosts are imposters fabricated by the devil. Neither would they think it probable that they are souls on leave from purgatory.

But the basic question remains: Are some ghosts returning spirits? And if they are, where are they returning from and how do they manage to do it?

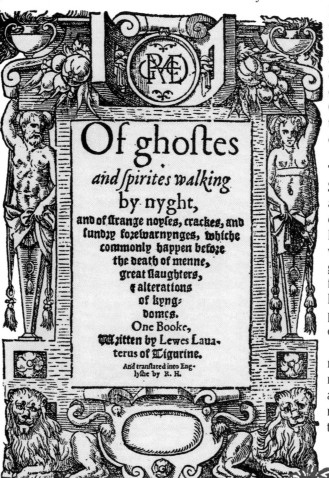

Attacking ghosts
The title page (above) of Louis Lavater's Of Ghostes and Spirites Walking by Nyght (*1572*). *A 17th-century engraving of the devil (right). Lavater argued that the devil was responsible for ghostly appearances.*

should like to be with you often on the voyage, for the love of adventure alone.' He again doffed his red cap, and disappeared as mysteriously as he came." Slocum awoke with the feeling that he had been in the presence of a friend and a seaman of vast experience and knowledge.

This story illustrates many of the paradoxes that have baffled attempts to explain the ghost experience. In the first place, there is only Slocum's word that anything happened at all. It is perfectly possible that he fabricated the entire story in order to make his book more exciting. Or again, supposing something really did happen, it is impossible to gauge the level of reality at which it happened. The pilot's second visit seems to have been a dream; perhaps the first was also? Was it just chance that the *Spray* held so surely to her course? Or did Slocum get to his feet and make the necessary arrangements without being conscious of what he was doing?

With so many unanswered questions, and in the absence of other witnesses, skeptics may be justified in suggesting that the entire ghost episode was a figment of Captain Slocum's imagination.

Practical purpose

But if so, skeptics must also account for the fact that the experience served a very practical purpose. If Slocum's imagination was responsible, what extraordinary psychological process was at work? If he had been visited by a guardian angel, it could be attributed to

Kindred spirits
An engraving depicting Christopher Columbus, the pioneering navigator, alone on his ship among the mysterious creatures that were thought to inhabit unknown waters. Lone sailor Joshua Slocum claimed that, while he lay unconscious below deck, the ghost of one of Columbus's crew steered his ship safely through a raging storm.

religious expectation; if the figure had been a devil or demon, again an explanation might be found in terms of traditional belief. But Slocum's ghost was not a folklore figure, but a historical one. Sailing the Atlantic, it is only natural that Slocum's thoughts would turn to the most famous of transatlantic sailors, and the pilot of the *Pinta* would be a natural guide in such an emergency situation. But that does not explain what complex thought process brought the pilot to the wheel of the *Spray*, nor what happened that night while Slocum lay helpless on the floor of his cabin and his boat sailed safely through the darkness. Here, surely, is the principal dilemma of the ghost experience: Why did it happen?

Profitable exercise

When that question is asked, it seems that ghost stories fall into two distinct categories, depending on who stands to profit by the experience. In some cases the benefit is on the ghost's side. Yet in Slocum's story, the incident seems to have occurred entirely for his benefit.

This seems to suggest that the skeptical view, that ghosts are a figment of the witness's imagination, may be only partially true. While it is possible to accept that Slocum's visitor may have been a creation of his own mind, there is a deeper mystery to be explained — the mystery of how the boat survived the night. Does this mean that there might be more than one kind of ghost, if they exist at all? On the one hand, ghosts like Captain Slocum's, which originate in the mind of the witness, and on the other, ghosts that visit us from some other sphere of reality?

Sinister spirit
Eskimo belief holds that ghosts are hostile to the living. As a result, Eskimo carvings, such as this one from northern Alaska, depict spirits as being particularly gruesome in appearance.

Spirits from the next world

In the cultures of primitive peoples, ghosts are synonymous with spirits from another level of reality — they are either human beings who once lived on earth but who have died and now inhabit a spirit world, or demons and spirits from that spirit world who for reasons of their own appear on earth. In such cultures, the spirit world is an accepted part of the scheme of things, so that the ghost experience is an accepted part of human experience.

This notion of the ghost as a spirit of the dead, leading an independent existence in some other sphere, has provided a possible explanation for ghosts throughout history. Because the idea has a certain inherent plausibility, it has been readily accepted as the basis for reports of ghost sightings: the "spirit

Shakespeare's spirit
An early 20th-century lantern slide depicts the dramatic moment when Macbeth is visited by Banquo's ghost.

> ## "He saw the murder'd person standing as a witness, ready to be examined against him, and ready to shew his throat which was cut by the prisoner."
>
> **Daniel Defoe, *The Secrets of the Invisible World Disclos'd***

of the dead" explanation is probably the one that most people — even today — would suggest in the first instance.

The alternative possibility, that some ghosts originate in the mind of the witness, is at least as old as the time of William Shakespeare. In his play, *Macbeth*, Shakespeare described how

the ghost of the murdered Banquo returned to haunt his doomed hero. There is a strong implication that Banquo's ghost is a projection from Macbeth's guilt-ridden mind.

English author, Daniel Defoe, writing a century later, was in no doubt about the status of ghosts. He was fascinated by ghosts, and his book *The Secrets of the Invisible World Disclos'd* (1735) is one of the first to take a refreshingly commonsense view of the subject. Defoe tells this story: "I have heard a story which I believe to be true, of a certain man who was brought to the bar of justice on suspicion of murder, which however he knew it was not in the power of human knowledge to detect. He pleaded *Not guilty*, and the court began to be at a loss for a proof, nothing but suspicion and circumstances appearing.

Phantom witness

"When the court thought they had no more witnesses to examine, and the man in a few moments would have been acquitted: he gave a start at the bar, as if he was frighted; but recovering his courage a little, he stretches out his arm towards the place where the witnesses usually stood, and pointing with his hand, My Lord, says he, that is not fair, tis not according to law.

"The court could not understand what the man meant, but Hold, says the Judge, the man sees something more than we do....and exhorted him to confess his crime. Upon this the self-condemn'd murderer burst out into tears and made a full confession of his crime: and gave the reasons of his being under such a

Spectral evidence
In this 18th-century illustration of a story from Daniel Defoe's The Secrets of the Invisible World Disclos'd, *the ghost of a murder victim confronts his killer in court.*

▶ PAGE 32

MOVING ON

Popular beliefs suggest that when we die we become spirits, joining the dead, and sometimes other nonhuman entities, in various other realms.

FROM HUMANKIND'S EARLIEST DAYS most societies have believed in some kind of other world to which people go when they depart from this life. For the most primitive peoples, the grave was the dead person's home, where he or she continued to live. This concept led to the idea of an underground kingdom, where the dead of many generations formed a subterranean community of their own. Living so close to the scenes of their earthly life, it was thought to be a simple matter for them to return. Since they were feared by the living, some societies placated them to discourage visiting, others took steps to force them to remain in the underworld.

Diverse locations

Gradually this notion was replaced by the idea that only the physical remains of the dead were left in the grave, while the real person — the spirit or soul, perceived variously by different cultures — departed, either immediately or as the body decomposed. For some, the spirit went with the sun to a region of the blessed in the west; for others it was located underground, under the sea, or in the sky. In North America the Tlingit Indians conceived of a "Ghosts' Home," and the Zunis a "Dance Village." In South Africa the Basuto heaven, Mosima, represented "the abyss" under the ground, while the islanders of New Caledonia, due to their close contact with the sea, believed that their particular spirit world, which was known as Tsiabiloum, existed beneath the ocean.

The reality of death

Though the physical body was left behind in the grave, the spirits who went on to inhabit these heavens kept their human appearance more or less, though

Chinese charm
The malevolent spirits of the dead were often thought to be kept at bay by religious charms. This Chinese amulet was supposed to defend against evil ghosts.

Life in paradise
A 15th-century Italian interpretation of a gardenlike paradise, taken from an illuminated manuscript.

Underworld afterlife
The islanders of New Caledonia in the Pacific anticipate an afterlife under the ocean. This carved and braided mask represents an inhabitant of their watery spirit world, known as Tsiabiloum.

Buddhist hell
A scene of hellish punishments from a fresco showing the Ten Courts of Hell. This fresco is found in the Tiger Balm Gardens in Hong Kong.

Eternal damnation
17th-century Flemish artist David Ryckaert produced this horrific vision of the entrance to Christian hell in "The Gates of Hades."

sometimes they changed for the worse. The Romans were apt to refer to the dead as *deformes*, the deformed ones, and the Egyptians believed that their spirits took horrific forms.

But deformed or not, these spirits were real. Christianity, too, teaches that the spirits of the dead are indeed real. The doctrine of the resurrection holds that the bodies of the dead will rise at the Last Judgment and, combined with their spirits, will continue to exist in the most literal sense.

Pleasure resorts

Gradually it came to be supposed that some of us, at least, can progress to a happier fate. The notion of separate arrangements for those who have behaved well during their lifetime and those who have not was a natural development. Among the Greeks, the favored dead went to the Elysian Fields and the less fortunate were condemned to Hades. These places could on occasion be visited by the living. The Muslim Paradise is no less literal, the ultimate pleasure resort, where the faithful will enjoy an unending existence of sensual fulfillment. By contrast, infidels and wrongdoers, in Islamic thinking as in many other creeds, can expect to suffer an eternity of pain and wretchedness in a variety of different hells.

Some religions, however, stopped short of condemning the dead to irrevocable damnation. It was supposed that those who had not behaved too terribly during their lifetime would go to an intermediate region — such as the Christian purgatory — where souls would have a second chance of qualifying for heaven.

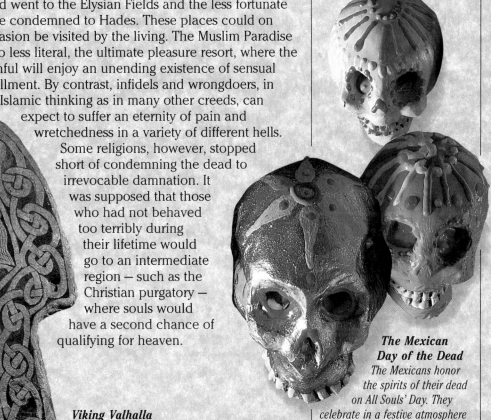

The Mexican Day of the Dead
The Mexicans honor the spirits of their dead on All Souls' Day. They celebrate in a festive atmosphere with traditional trappings, such as these sugar skulls.

Viking Valhalla
Norse heroes went to Valhalla, generally conceived of as a vast drinking-hall where Vikings spend eternity imbibing and telling boastful tales of their mighty deeds. This eighth-century stone picture, from Gotland in Sweden, depicts a scene in Valhalla in which a dead Viking warrior on horseback is offered a drink.

RESCUE ATTEMPTS

There have been many stories about attempts to rescue spirits from their twilight world. The folklorist Lewis Spence, in his *Myths of the North American Indians* (1914), tells the story of Sayadio, a young Iroquois of the Wyandot tribe, who resolved to bring his sister back from the Land of Spirits. He searched for many years until he finally encountered "the keeper of the

Orpheus and Eurydice

Spirit-land," who gave him a magic gourd with which to catch his sister's spirit. Eventually Sayadio was successful, but an inquisitive Indian girl could not resist peeping into the gourd — and the sister's spirit flew to freedom.

Sayadio's story has a similar theme to the tale of Orpheus and Eurydice. The Greek hero Orpheus was inconsolable when his wife, Eurydice, died. He found her spirit with the ghosts of the dead in Hades, and was allowed to lead her back to the land of the living on condition that he did not look at her. But doubt took hold, and as Orpheus turned he saw his wife disappear forever.

surprise, *viz*, that he saw the murder'd person standing as a witness, ready to be examined against him, and ready to shew his throat which was cut by the prisoner."

By way of comment, Defoe says there was no real apparition, no specter, no ghost or appearance. He claims "it was all figur'd out to him by the power of his own guilt, and the agitations of his soul."

Defoe insists that in such cases, the soul of the murdered person does not seek revenge. Instead, it is to the soul of the murderer that we must look for the origin of the incident.

Defoe took the same view of what is probably the most frequently recorded type of ghost story, the crisis apparition, in which a ghost is seen at the same time that an accident is occurring to the person it resembles. Defoe tells of Lady Osborne, who was visited by the apparition of her husband in their country house, at the exact moment he died in the West Indies. The dead man reproached her for her extravagant lifestyle and warned her to change her ways. Moreover, the same apparition was reported to have appeared previously to a servant girl in his London house, taking the form of someone pretending to want to rent an apartment in the house.

A skeptical view

Defoe invites the reader to share his skepticism that, at the moment of his death, when his mind was surely occupied with weightier matters, Sir John Osborne would stop at the London house, assume a shape for that purpose, talk about the most frivolous things with Mary the maid, and then go with another formal errand to Lady Osborne. And having dispatched these more weighty affairs, he would then go on to Heaven afterward.

However, Defoe does leave several awkward questions unanswered. First, there is the fact that the apparition was

seen both by the servant girl and by Lady Osborne. There is also the coincidence of the apparitions with the time of Sir John's death — these are aspects of the story which are not easily explained.

Then again, Mary had never seen her master, and did not recognize the apparition. Yet when she compared her visitor with Lady Osborne's, it seemed clear to the two women that they had both been visited by the same person. How could Mary have invented such an apparition? On the other hand, if Defoe's suggestion that the whole business originated in Lady Osborne's mind is correct, then what is the meaning of the apparition to the servant girl?

Such puzzles and paradoxes are characteristic of what is probably the

> ## She thought his behavior strange and asked if he felt all right? He turned to face her — and instead of George's face she saw a strange white death-mask.

most frequent of all kinds of ghost story, that of apparitions at the moment of death. What follows is from the October 1957 edition of the American magazine *Fate*, and is a typical example.

Apparition of death

"Mary Travers was sitting up late waiting for her husband George, an insurance salesman, to return home. She heard the clock strike 11 P.M.; then, some time later, she heard a cab coming down the street and stopping in front of the house. She heard a voice, presumably the driver's, call out 'Good night!' and heard her husband's familiar steps on the porch. She hurried to let him in: he entered silently, his hat pulled low over his eyes, and stood with his back to Mary while she closed the door. She thought his behavior strange and asked if he felt all right? He turned to face her — and instead of George's face she saw a strange white death-mask. She screamed, which brought the neighbors hurrying in; the apparition disappeared. Minutes later the phone rang to say that George had been killed in a train crash."

However much Defoe's all-in-the-mind explanation might be attractive, it is really easier to account for this story in what might be called spirit-of-the-dead terms. There was no reason for Mrs. Travers to be particularly apprehensive, apart from the usual concern of a wife for her husband. Why would she suddenly imagine his sinister apparition, on the very night when there really were grounds for her fears? It makes better sense to speculate that the ghost might have been some form of projection from George's mind, sent through space to tell his wife what had happened.

Video evidence?

The various types of ghost story do have one thing in common, and that is that every ghost must have a witness. This leads to the question: Can ghosts appear without a witness? Many attempts have been made to "catch" ghosts with video cameras: and if ever such an event is successful, a number of interesting questions would be raised. But thus far good ghost videos exist only in the films.

For the time being, however, there is no reason to suppose that ghosts appear, if they do at all, independently of a human witness. Consequently it may be possible to theorize that the witness may be necessary for the manifestation of a ghost to take place, even in those cases where it does not seem likely that the witness is the cause of the apparition.

Psychic sensitivity

In many cases the witness appears to be the driving force. An example is the account of Captain Slocum and the pilot of the *Pinta*. But even in those instances where the ghost seems to have an external source, it seems likely that the witness plays more than a passive part. Perhaps, in speculative terms, he or she provides something like psychic energy that enables the manifestation to occur.

If some people possess more of this power or sensitivity than others — which is perhaps the same thing as saying that they are more receptive to psychic events — this might explain why some people see ghosts while others do not.

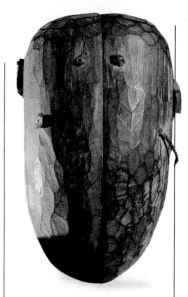

Tsimshian owl
This wooden heart, carved by the Tsimshian Indians of the Pacific Northwest, opens to reveal an owl. These Indians believe that the souls of the recently dead turn into owls.

FACT OR FOLKLORE?

Many of the ghost stories told over the ages bear a remarkable resemblance to one another. This observation leads to the possibility that what is presented as an individual experience may in fact be a communal experience — that is to say, a piece of folklore.

Popular legends

The dividing line between ghost stories and folklore is vague and uncertain. Without knowing more about how ghosts are seen, it is impossible to tell how certain stories come to be told over and over again, until they are classed as folklore. In some cases, what appear to be individual histories are in fact popular legends that the storyteller has "borrowed." But it does not automatically follow that the individual histories have no basis in fact. English investigator Michael Goss researched the classic folklore phenomenon of the "phantom hitchhiker," a story in which a truck driver picks up a hitchhiker, only to discover later that his passenger had died in an auto accident several years before. Goss was disconcerted to find that, on some occasions at least, there seemed to be a factual basis for the story in real-life experience.

Michael Goss's findings lead to the paradoxical situation in which, while it is likely that most folklore legends originate as fireside tales or popular rumors, some of them may actually point to real-life scenarios which are perhaps modeled on the legend.

More often, no doubt, the borrowing is deliberate, a conscious act on the part of the storyteller to impress his or her listeners or simply for the fun of it. In other cases, however, it seems that the individuals who tell a folk legend as if it came from personal experience have come honestly to believe that the event really happened to them.

Borrowing from fiction

How can this be? Surely people know whether they are lying? For most people, perhaps, this is true; but it seems that there is a small percentage of the population for whom the dividing line between fact and fantasy is so vague as to be virtually nonexistent. And this is something to keep in mind when looking at the varieties of ghost stories being told. It is important to remember that with all ghostly tales there is always the possibility that the account is not someone's personal experience, but a popular legend that the teller has appropriated, consciously or unconsciously, for himself or herself.

Childhood friends
A little girl greets her fantasy friends on this book cover from the 1920's.

IMAGINARY COMPANIONS
Characteristic of fantasy-prone behavior is the tendency in childhood to create make-believe "companions." In her book *My Life* (1938), psychic Eileen Garrett tells how, when she was four years old, she first met her imaginary playmates: "There were two little girls and a boy. I first saw them framed in the doorway; they were strange to me, as were all children. I longed to play with them....

"Out-of-doors next day, I saw them again. I joined them, and after that they came to see me daily. Sometimes they stayed all day, sometimes but a little while....

"I never doubted the reality of 'My Children.' I touched them and they were soft and warm."

What all of these stories have in common is that living people have a clear feeling of seeing, and in some cases interacting with, a being or thing that can be shown not to be physically present — either because it is dead, or because it is known to be located elsewhere at the time, or because the circumstances make it clear that this is not reality as we understand it.

Fantastic experiences
However, while the witness may find the experience impressive, others are not likely to feel quite the same way unless they share it — and this happens only in a small minority of cases. There is always the suspicion that the witness is fantasizing.

There is reason to believe that a certain proportion of people are "fantasy prone" — that is, they are inclined to

> "Quick as a flash I turned and distinctly saw the form of my dead sister, and for a brief second or so looked her squarely in the face."

suppose things to be real which in fact, by the standards of everyday judgment, are only imaginary.

Could all ghosts be fantasies of this kind? It is hard to believe the theory, for that is all it is, could account for more than a small proportion of cases. In particular, the "fantasy" theory would have to be stretched to an excessive degree to account for those cases in which information, unknown to the witness, is provided by the ghost.

Consider, for example, this famous case, one that was reported to the British Society for Psychical Research by Mr. F. G.,

Eileen Garrett
Irish psychic Garrett claimed that she played with her childhood fantasy friends on and off for nine years.

of Boston, Massachusetts, in 1888: "In 1867 my only sister, a young lady of 18 years, died suddenly of cholera, in St. Louis, Missouri. My attachment for her was very strong, and the blow a severe one to me. A year or so after her death, I became a commercial traveller, and it was in 1876 while on one of my Western trips that the event occurred."

Brotherly love
Mr. F. G. claimed that he had "drummed" the city of St. Joseph, Missouri, and had gone to his room at the Pacific House hotel to send in his orders. Because he had secured an unusually large number of sales that morning, he said he was in a very happy frame of mind.

He went on to relate what happened next: "My thoughts, of course, were about these orders. I had not been thinking of my late sister, or in any manner reflecting on the past. The hour was high noon, and the sun was shining cheerfully into my room. While busily smoking a cigar, and writing out my orders, I suddenly became conscious that someone was sitting on my left, with one arm resting on the table. Quick as a flash I turned and distinctly saw the form of my dead sister, and for a brief second or so looked her squarely in the face."

Mr. F. G. said that he was absolutely certain that it was indeed his sister he saw. Calling out her name in delight, he jumped up to greet her. However, at that very moment, he later claimed, her apparition instantly vanished.

Vivid vision
"Naturally I was startled and dumbfounded," he continued, "almost doubting my senses; but the cigar in my mouth, and pen in hand, with the ink still moist on my letter, satisfied me that I had not been dreaming, and was wide awake. I was near enough to touch her, had it been a physical possibility, and noted her features, expression, and details of dress. She appeared as if alive. Her eyes looked kindly and perfectly natural into mine. Her skin was so lifelike that I could see the glow of moisture on its surface.

"Now comes the most remarkable confirmation of my statement. This visitation, or whatever you may call it, so impressed me that I took the next train

home, and in the presence of my parents and others I related what had occurred. My father, a man of rare good sense and very practical, was inclined to ridicule me; but he too was amazed when later on I told them of a bright red line or scratch on the right-hand side of my sister's face, which I distinctly had seen.

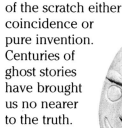

St. Joseph, Missouri, c. 1865
It was in the Pacific House hotel in this southern town that Mr. F. G. claims to have seen an apparition of his dead sister.

"When I mentioned this, my mother rose trembling to her feet and nearly fainted away, and as soon as she sufficiently recovered her self-possession, with tears streaming down her face, she exclaimed

> ## "My mother rose trembling to her feet...she exclaimed that I had indeed seen my sister, as no living mortal but herself was aware of that scratch."

that I had indeed seen my sister, as no living mortal but herself was aware of that scratch, which she had accidentally made while doing some little act of kindness after my sister's death. She said she well remembered how pained she was to think she should have, unintentionally, marred the features of her dead daughter, and that, unknown to all, she had carefully obliterated all traces of the slight scratch with the aid of powder, etc, and that she had never mentioned it to a single human being, from that day to this."

Looking for the truth

This case presents the fundamental question of the ghost experience: what had Mr. F. G. seen? Had he seen a mental image, which had been produced in some manner by his own mind, and supplemented by information known only to his mother? Or could it have been an image projected by his sister herself? If this was possible, and clearly it is not proven, then, where was she projecting it from? Was she still "alive" on some other level of existence that we cannot comprehend?

If asked, a spiritualist would doubtless answer that yes, the sister was and is still living, though not the same kind of life as she lived on earth, and not in any spatial dimension we know of. Whereas a skeptic would surely argue that the vision was purely the result of wishful thinking on the part of the bereaved brother, and the detail of the scratch either coincidence or pure invention. Centuries of ghost stories have brought us no nearer to the truth.

Spirit abodes
The natives of the island of New Ireland, in the Bismarck Archipelago in the Pacific, carved chalk figures such as these in the belief that they would become homes for the spirits of their deceased forebears.

COMPACT CASES

In an effort to solve the mysteries of ghosts and the spirit world, some people have taken a practical step. In "compact" cases, two friends agree that whichever of them dies first will attempt to return and communicate with the remaining survivor.

COMPACT CASE STORIES have been told for centuries. As early as 1709 the Italian historian Cesare Baronius wrote of a compact between two Latin scholars, in his work *De Apparitionibus Mortuorum, Vivis et Pacto Factis:* "These two illustrious friends, Michael Mercatus and Marcellinus Ficinus, after a long discourse on the nature of the soul, had agreed that, if possible, whichever died first should return to visit the other. Some time afterward, while Mercatus was engaged in study at an early hour in the morning, he suddenly heard the noise of a horse galloping in the street, which presently stopped at his door, and the voice of his friend Ficinus exclaimed: 'Oh Michael, Oh Michael, those things are true!' Whereupon Mercatus hastily opened his window, and espied his friend Ficinus on a white steed."

Life of religious study

Mercatus called out after his friend, but apparently Ficinus had galloped away. On sending to Florence to inquire after him, he learnt that Ficinus had died about the time he had seen him. From that period onward, Mercatus dedicated his life to religious study.

Another case is reported from the 17th century, when two French students, Bezuel and Desfontaines, made a similar agreement and signed it in blood. A year or so later, while working in the fields, Bezuel was seen to stop work and walk some 30 paces away down a lane. There, he seemed to be talking to an invisible person, for nearly an hour. On his return, he told his friends that he had been talking to Desfontaines, who had

> "We actually committed the folly of drawing up an agreement, written in our blood...that whichever of us died the first should appear to the other...."

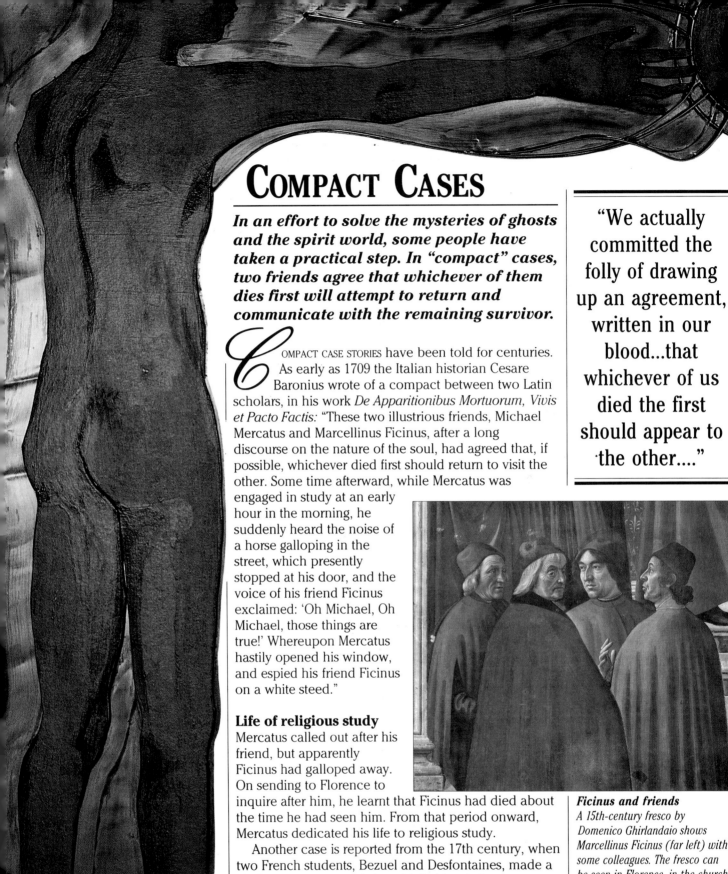

Ficinus and friends
A 15th-century fresco by Domenico Ghirlandaio shows Marcellinus Ficinus (far left) with some colleagues. The fresco can be seen in Florence, in the church of Sta. Maria Novella.

drowned the previous day while bathing in the river at Caen. He had named his companions, and gave a detailed description of the events. Pierre Le Loyer discusses the case in his book *Discourse on Spectres, Visions and Apparitions of Spirits* (1608), and assumes that the details were accurate.

The best-known of these cases is that of Lord Brougham, a distinguished 19th-century British statesman, who made a compact with his college friend Geoffrey Garner. "We frequently discussed and speculated upon many grave subjects," said Brougham, "among others, on the immortality of the soul, and on a future state. This question, and the possibility, I will not say of ghosts walking, but of the dead appearing to the living, were subjects of much speculation: and we actually committed the folly of drawing up an agreement, written in our blood, to the effect that whichever of us died the first should appear to the other, and thus solve any doubts we had entertained of the 'life after death.'"

Lord Henry Brougham

Holiday visit
When they left college, Garner obtained a government posting in India, and over the years the two friends gradually lost touch. Many years later, when Brougham was traveling in Sweden, he related the following extraordinary tale: "Arriving at a decent inn, we decided to stop for the night. I was glad to take advantage of a hot bath before I turned in, and here a most remarkable thing happened to me....I turned my head round...as I was about to get out of the bath. On the chair sat Garner, looking calmly at me."

Familiar apparition
"How I got out of the bath I know not," Brougham continued, "but on recovering my senses I found myself sprawling on the floor. The apparition, or whatever it was, that had taken the likeness of Garner, had disappeared."

Returning home, Brougham learned that Garner had died in India on December 19, the date he saw the apparition. Many years later he seemed skeptical. "The number of coincidences between the vision and the event," he wrote, "are perhaps fewer and less remarkable than a fair calculation of chances would warrant us to expect. I believe every such seeming miracle is, like every ghost story, capable of explanation."

Other commentators, too, have ascribed such cases to coincidence, but how often can the remarkable synchronicity of such experiences be ignored? Discussing the compact cases collected in *Phantasms of the Living*, the British Society for Psychical Research found nine examples of an apparition following on a compact of this kind, and the authors disagree with Brougham. "Considering what an extremely small number of persons make such a compact," they wrote, "it is difficult to resist the conclusion that its existence has a certain efficacy."

INANIMATE GHOSTS

Most phantoms resemble people. But there are many reports of inanimate ghosts, such as ships, trains, trucks, and even houses, that cannot easily be explained in spiritual terms.

IN A BOOK OF LETTERS ENTITLED *Notes & Queries* (1860), Edmund Lenthal Swifte, keeper of the crown jewels in the Tower of London from 1814 to 1852, described a bizarre apparition. One evening in October 1817 Swifte was having supper with his family. The doors were closed, the windows curtained; two candles on the table lit the room.

"I had offered a glass of wine and water to my wife," Swifte recounted, "when, on putting it to her lips, she paused and exclaimed: 'What is that?' I looked up and saw a cylindrical figure, like a glass tube, seemingly about the thickness of my arm, and hovering between the ceiling and the table; its contents appeared to be a dense fluid, white and pale azure...and incessantly mingling within the cylinder."

Hovering tube

Swifte claimed that the tube hovered there for about two minutes, before it slowly moved toward his sister-in-law, and then positioned itself in front of his son and himself. It then paused for a moment over his wife's right shoulder, and even though she could not see it, she crouched down, and covering her shoulder with both hands, shrieked: "It has seized me!"

Swifte declared: "Even now, while writing, I feel the fresh horror of that moment. I caught up my chair... rushed upstairs to the children's room, and told the terrified nurse what I had seen. Meanwhile the other domestics had hurried into the parlour, where their mistress recounted to them the scene...." Curiously enough, though both Swifte and his wife said they saw the apparition, their son and Swifte's sister-in-law did not. This led him to suppose that it must have been a supernatural

The Martin Tower
A 19th-century engraving showing the tower where Edmund Lenthal Swifte held office as keeper of the crown jewels.

phenomenon of some kind, but whatever it was, its purpose seemed to be as obscure as its appearance.

A cylindrical UFO?
Somewhat similar objects seen in the second half of the 20th century are described as unidentified flying objects (UFO's), and one theory is that they might be caused by ball lightning. But the object seen by Mr. and Mrs. Swifte seems to have been too artificially structured to be a natural object.

Yet can it possibly be classified as a ghost? The author Christina Hole includes it in her book *Haunted England* (1940), but somewhat uneasily.

Stories of inanimate objects such as phantom coaches, trains, and ships, somehow seem easier to comprehend. In

It paused for a moment over his wife's right shoulder....She crouched down and shrieked: "It has seized me!"

a letter published in *The Occult Review* in June 1921, Mr. F. G. Montagu Powell tells of an incident that occurred in July 1859 when, as a youth, he was serving with the Royal Navy. He was the midshipman of the watch on H.M.S. *Euryalus* off the Cape of Good Hope when at about 11 A.M., he observed a dull and heavy mist falling over the ship.

Spectral ship
He related what happened next: "We sighted a sailing ship right ahead of us, lying in fact right across our track and so close that before we could hail her or alter our course we were on top of her and in fact cut clean through her....Her sails seemed to me flat, lifeless and discoloured, no 'bellying to the breeze' about them. Her crew, clad in sou'westers and tarpaulins and the traditional breeches, moved lifelessly about the decks, coiling up ropes or leaning over the hammock netting, and paying not the slightest attention to us." Montagu Powell said that the vessel appeared to suffer no damage, but

SPECTRAL COACH

The phantom coach has a special place in English folklore. In *Haunted England* (1940) Christina Hole writes: "There is scarcely an old road in England along which the Spectral Coach has not trundled at some time or another. It may be either a genuine coach or a hearse; but whatever form it takes, it bears certain distinguishing marks which prove it to be something from another world. It is always black, and so are the driver and his horses. Often both are headless. It appears suddenly on the roadway and moves very fast and usually without noise. Only in a few cases do we hear of the rumble of wheels on the road or the clattering of horses' hoofs to give warning of its approach. Like most apparitions of its kind, it is an ominous thing to meet, and serves as a death-omen for those unlucky enough to encounter it."

Keynsham railway station
This old photograph of the station gives an impression of how the phantom engine seen by railway workers might have looked as it swept silently toward the fateful tunnel.

simply vanished in the mist. He went on to ask: "Do I believe it, or was it mirage, or is it a youthful dream called up by the associations of the Cape and the story attached to it?"

Certainly the story brings to mind the legend of the famous phantom ship, the *Flying Dutchman*. It has been claimed that this legend may have originated with a person rather than a ship. It may have begun with the misdeeds of a certain captain Hendrik Vanderdecken, who blasphemed against God and was supposedly condemned to sail the seas in a phantom ship until the Last Judgment. But does Montagu Powell's spectral ship fall into the same category?

Ghostly trains

Railway ghosts are more frequent, and whole books have been devoted to them alone. Phantom trains have been reported on many occasions. One such is a railway porter's account recorded by Irish ghost-hunter Elliott O'Donnell in the August 1930 edition of *The Occult Review*. The porter said that, when on duty at Keynsham station near Bristol, England, he, together with one or two of the other porters, had repeatedly seen a phantom engine passing through the

H.M.S. Euryalus

station in the direction of the tunnel farther down the railway line.

They claimed that the engine would suddenly appear, and pass swiftly and noiselessly through the station. The driver would turn slowly round and look at the men on the platform with a pale face and troubled expression. Sometimes the phenomenon occurred at night, sometimes in broad daylight. It was rumored that either a driver or fireman had been killed in the tunnel under strange circumstances, and the phantom engine was thought to have appeared after that tragedy.

Churchyard companion

Phantom vehicles are extraordinary enough, but the ghost is even more remarkable when it takes the form of a building. In 1953 *Fate* magazine ran a feature about a phantom one-story house that octogenarian Luther Suthers claimed he saw during the spring of 1953. The setting was Crown City, Ohio, in an area of broad lawn adjacent to the Methodist church. Suthers, who lived about 100 yards from the church grounds, said he saw the house on a number of occasions over a six-week period before he dared to mention it to anyone.

Moving house

He claimed it was always the same, with a 10-foot bush in front of it, right in the middle of the church lawn. Sometimes it was there and sometimes it wasn't. Often it dissolved or moved away as Suthers watched it. He looked at it with one eye closed. He tried the other eye. Finally he was convinced he was seeing something.

Nobody quite believed Luther Suthers, attributing his alleged sightings to the vagaries of old age. But not long after, as two other townspeople, Garfield Watts and H. S. Gilkerson, were leaving a

◆ PAGE 42

GHOSTLY TRUCK

"I drive a trailer and haul produce from Florida up the East Coast....For the past year and a half...a phantom truck follows me at least part of the time."

*P*HANTOM COACHES appear to have developed a modern counterpart in the form of phantom trucks. Writing in *Fate* in 1986, truck driver Harriette Spanabel of Brooksville, Florida, told of an experience that calls to mind Steven Spielberg's haunting movie *Duel* (1971): "I drive a tractor trailer and haul produce from Florida up the East Coast and west as far as Texas. For the past year and a half, always on my return run, a phantom truck follows me at least part of the time. At first I thought it was my imagination. One minute nothing would be behind me but the next minute a tractor trailer would be there."

Mysterious tail

Spanabel claims that the truck usually appeared at night. She said that a friend, Kelly Rose, had also witnessed the mystery truck, and described a journey the two friends took in March 1985. "It was when we were coming back from Miami that the truck first joined us at approximately 11:30 the evening of the 12th. I drove out of Lakeland, Florida, on U.S. 98 going north. I planned to turn on to S.R. 471 which runs through the middle of the

Green Swamp. The phantom truck first appeared behind us on U.S. 98 about two miles before I made my turn onto S.R. 471. It followed us from there until we had almost reached S.R. 50 where I go west....

"On a narrow two-lane road which runs through a state forest, about 50 miles from my house, the truck again appeared behind us. Kelly immediately asked where it had come from. Of course I couldn't tell her, but it followed us for 30 miles before it disappeared this time. Kelly, who had been watching the truck intently in her mirror, was astounded. I stopped my truck on 471 and we got out and looked for the other truck. It was completely gone. On this road there are no side roads [and] no shoulders where a truck could pull off without either tipping over or ending up tangled in a mass of big trees. And let me add there was no other traffic on 471 going either direction."

Out to lunch
Staff at the Bridge Lunch restaurant in the 1950's, ready for the lunchtime session.

PHANTOM TRAIN
John Quirk of Pittsfield, Massachusetts, reported that he and several customers at the Bridge Lunch diner saw a phantom train one afternoon in February 1958. He described the train, which comprised a baggage car and five or six coaches, in great detail; he said he could even see the coal in the tender. A month later a similar train passed at full steam, highballing toward Boston at 6:30 in the morning.

Railway officials pointed out that no steam engine had run on that line for years. On another specific occasion when the phantom train was reported, the officials were able to confirm that no train of any kind had passed along the tracks at that time.

mid-week church service late at night, they too saw the house. It was a two-story house this time, but both swore they spotted it at the same time, and as they started toward it, it drifted away.

Nonrevealing records
Research from historical records revealed that no house had ever been built on the site. But Luther Suthers, Garfield Watts, and H. S. Gilkerson were convinced that there had been a house there — even if it had been only a phantom one.

And if a phantom house makes heavy demands on credulity, what about an entire phantom landscape? Cecil Edward Denny, while serving with the Northwest Mounted Police in Alberta, Canada, in 1875, was traveling alone by boat down Oldman River, in wild mountain country, when he was caught in a thunderstorm. In his book, *Riders of the Plains* (1905), he wrote the following account: "I found it impossible to make my way, and I determined to land and wait until the storm was over. I saw on the south bank a good clump of timber, and determined to take shelter in it. As I approached, the fury of the storm for a moment abated, and I could plainly hear the drums beating in an Indian camp, and the sound of the Indian 'Hi-ya' mingling with it."

Seeking shelter
Believing he had stumbled on an Indian camp where he could take refuge from the storm, Denny landed and made his way on foot as quickly as possible through the wood in the direction of the

sounds. Despite the ferocious rain and lightning, he battled his way into an open glade where he saw "before me the Indian camp not more than two hundred yards away. I could see men and women, and even children, moving about among the lodges. This surprised me, as you do not often find the Indians moving about in the wet if they can help it."

Denny estimated that there were about 20 lodges in the camp, and just as he was considering which one to make for, he said he suddenly seemed surrounded by a blaze of lightning. At the same time a crash of thunder followed, and he noticed a large tree not far off had been

> "A few minutes before not only a large Indian camp had stood there, and the voices of the Indians could be distinctly heard, but now all had suddenly disappeared."

struck. He reported what happened next: "I was fortunate to have escaped with my life, and, as it was, it was a few minutes before I was able to rise and look around. I looked towards the place

Mounties and Indians
Cecil Edward Denny saw a phantom Indian camp while serving with the Mounties. Here he is pictured (far left) with fellow constables and Indian interpreters.

where the camp stood, but to my unutterable astonishment as well as terror, it was not there. It was quite light, although still storming heavily, and was not much after four o'clock.

Overwhelming terror

"A few minutes before not only a large Indian camp had stood there, and the voices of the Indians could be distinctly heard, but now all had suddenly disappeared, even to the band of horses that were quietly grazing there only a few minutes before. I stood for a moment...when suddenly an over-whelming sense of terror seemed to seize me, and almost without knowing what I did, I ran."

Indian slaughter

The next morning, Denny returned to the site with an Indian and an interpreter. The area was deserted and there were no recent signs of habitation, but a few rings of stone partly overgrown with grass showed where an old camp had been situated years before. Questioning revealed that the Blackfeet had surprised and slaughtered a camp of Cree Indians on the site many years earlier.

In attempting to explain a case such as this, where the witness allegedly saw a whole village of people, it is helpful to suggest that some kind of mirage effect might have taken place. But the wealth of detail Denny provided suggests an alternative explanation: that he had seen a ghostly vision of the Cree village which had existed on the same site at some point in the past.

Different explanation

If Denny's and the other stories previously discussed were merely isolated cases, imagination or fabrication might explain them away. But there are many more such tales — many more phantom ships, coaches, and trains, many more visions of places that plainly do not physically exist in the form in which they are seen. This diversity of experience suggests, to some extent, that while some ghosts might be attributed to the traditional theories involving returning spirits of the dead, there may be many more accounts that demand an altogether different explanation.

FUTURE FLIGHT?

What possible explanation could there be for the sudden appearance of an entire airfield, stocked with machinery that had not even been invented?

IN SCOTLAND in 1935, Air Marshal Sir Victor Goddard (then a wing commander) of the Royal Air Force (RAF), was interested in the possibility of using the old First World War airfield at Drem, in Lothian, as an RAF training field. He visited the site and saw that the buildings were dilapidated and the landing field had been turned into farmland. Goddard decided that in its current state the site was unusable as an airfield at that time.

Lightning recovery

The following day, flying alone, he ran into bad weather, went into a spin, and nearly crashed. He fought to recover control of his aircraft, which he did successfully. Next, he had to ascertain his whereabouts; so he flew lower to look for a landmark and saw that he was close to Drem. Soon he was crossing the airfield boundary. The moment he did so, the rainstorm around him changed dramatically to bright sunlight. He saw the airfield, but was stunned to see that it was in full use. Four planes, painted bright yellow, were being serviced by mechanics in blue overalls and he was surprised to see that one of the aircraft was a monoplane. The hangars that Goddard had seen derelict the day before were now in good repair, as was the tarmac.

Flying only a few feet above the ground, his plane must have made a great deal of noise and yet, strangely, no one looked up.

Air Marshal Goddard

As he swooped low he passed once again from the sunlight back into the rain.

When Goddard recounted his adventure to his colleagues, he was laughed at and accused of drinking too much whisky. As a result he said no more about it. A few years later he heard that Drem had indeed been refurbished and opened as a training airfield. But he did not revisit it until 1964.

There are certain features of Goddard's story that suggest that it might have been some form of a vision of the future. No RAF aircraft was painted yellow until four years after the incident, there were no monoplanes in service in 1935, and blue overalls were not introduced until 1938. Yet stranger still is the fact that in Goddard's vision he had seen the existing hangars in good repair; in fact the old hangars were subsequently pulled down and replaced with a different design. So it seems unlikely that Drem airfield ever looked as it appeared to Goddard. The air marshal himself wonders whether his vision may have been a "precognition of ideas" — that is, he saw the airfield as someone may have imagined it, before it was rebuilt.

Monoplane before its time?

A Miles Magister two-seater training plane. Goddard saw a similar plane during his strange vision of Drem airfield, several years before this model was in service.

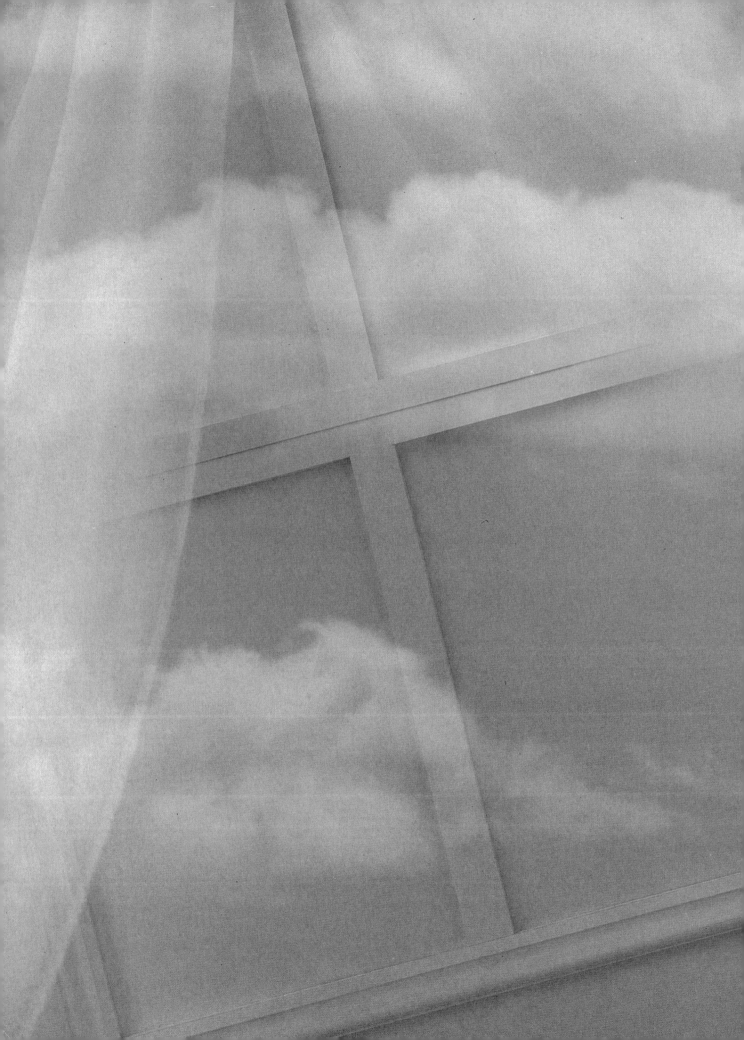

CHAPTER TWO

HAUNTED PLACES

Ghosts are most often reported to be haunting one particular place. Whether in the White House or on a Greek battlefield, such hauntings appear to signify the spirits' irresistible compulsion to return to the surroundings that were familiar to them in life.

When Queen Wilhelmina of the Netherlands was visiting the White House, as a guest of President Franklin D. Roosevelt, she stayed in the Lincoln Room. As she slept one night, the queen was awakened by a knock on the door. She gave permission for the caller to enter, but there was no reply. The knock was repeated. Finally, the queen climbed out of bed and opened the door. What she saw next made her faint and fall to the floor. For there before her, as she explained to Roosevelt the next morning,

PROPHETIC DREAM

Perhaps the best-known of Abraham Lincoln's various psychic experiences was the disturbing dream he had a few days before his assassination on April 15, 1865. He recounted this dream the following day to his secretary and friend, Ward Hill Lamon, who recorded it in his biography of the president, *The Life of Abraham Lincoln* (1872).

His dream, said Lincoln, took place in the White House, over which there seemed to hang a deathlike stillness. Wandering downstairs, Lincoln heard sobbing everywhere, but no one was to be seen. He kept on walking through the house until he arrived at the East Room, which he entered.

"Who is dead?"

"There I met with a sickening surprise," he said. "Before me was a catafalque, on which rested a corpse wrapped in funeral vestments. Around it were stationed soldiers who were acting as guards; and there was a throng of people, some gazing mournfully upon the corpse, whose face was covered, others weeping pitifully.

"'Who is dead in the White House?' I demanded of one of the soldiers. 'The President,' was his dramatic answer, 'he was killed by an assassin!'"

Lincoln was shot dead a few days later. His body lay in state in the East Room.

The Lincoln Room at the White House

stood the unmistakable figure of former president Abraham Lincoln, gravely doffing his characteristic stovepipe hat.

Roosevelt himself confided to Carl Sandburg, the poet and historian who wrote the biography *Abraham Lincoln: The War Years* (1940), that on a few occasions, when he had been alone in the Blue Room, he was convinced that Lincoln was there too. Roosevelt once told actor Frank Wilson: "The spirit of Lincoln still lives on here."

Footsteps and rappings

Other presidents, important visitors, and staff have helped support the belief that the White House is apparently haunted by the ghost of Lincoln. Even Winston Churchill, according to Susy Smith's book, *Prominent American Ghosts* (1967), saw a figure that resembled Abraham Lincoln.

Rumors began within months of the president's assassination in 1865, when several inhabitants of the building reported hearing mysterious footsteps and rappings with no visible source.

The first recorded occasion on which an apparition of Lincoln was supposedly seen was during the presidency of Calvin Coolidge (1923–29). Grace Coolidge, the

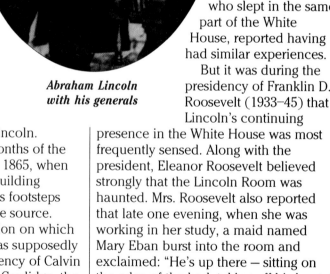

Abraham Lincoln with his generals

president's wife, claimed that she was in the Oval Room one day when she saw the figure of Lincoln standing at the window, gazing out in deep thought. And, in her book, *White House Profile* (1951), Bess Furman states that Theodore Roosevelt, president from 1901 to 1909, was aware of the ghostly presence of Lincoln's spirit.

Yet another president, Harry S. Truman, in office from 1945 to 1953, disclosed in 1956 that he had been awakened several times at night by knocks on his bedroom door, only to find that no one was there. His daughter, Margaret, who slept in the same part of the White House, reported having had similar experiences.

But it was during the presidency of Franklin D. Roosevelt (1933–45) that Lincoln's continuing presence in the White House was most frequently sensed. Along with the president, Eleanor Roosevelt believed strongly that the Lincoln Room was haunted. Mrs. Roosevelt also reported that late one evening, when she was working in her study, a maid named Mary Eban burst into the room and exclaimed: "He's up there — sitting on the edge of the bed, taking off his boots." When Mrs. Roosevelt asked who "he" was, the maid replied, "Mr. Lincoln!"

"That was Abe"

Another White House maid, Lillian Parks, remembered a day when the building was almost empty and she was in a room next to the Lincoln Room. Over and over she heard footsteps crossing the Lincoln Room floor. But whenever she looked in, there was no one there. After an hour she went upstairs and asked the house-man why he kept walking across that room. He replied that he had only just come on duty and had not been on that floor. "That was Abe you heard," he said.

Why should it be Lincoln's spirit, rather than that of any other president, that allegedly has been sensed, heard, or seen so often at the White House? Believers in ghosts suggest that the hauntings may be connected to the fact that in his lifetime Lincoln was far more interested and involved in spiritual matters than any other president. One example of this was revealed after the death of his 11-year-old son, Willie, in February 1862. The loss plunged Lincoln

---

Franklin D. Roosevelt once told actor Frank Wilson: "The spirit of Lincoln still lives on here."

---

into deep despair, but then one day, after listening to the condolences of a minister, the president suddenly exclaimed that he knew that Willie was still alive. And, in private conversation with the Secretary of the Treasury, Salmon P. Chase, he confided: "Ever since Willie's death I catch myself involuntarily talking to him as if he were with me — *and I feel that he is!*"

The medium is the message
Undoubtedly, it was a hope that he might communicate with his dead son that led Lincoln to attend various séances organized by Mrs. Lincoln at the White House. The young medium Nettie Colburn conducted a séance in December 1862. Lincoln, according to the medium's later account, listened spellbound as she delivered in a deep, trance-like voice a plea for the president to carry out his plans to emancipate America's slaves. According to Colburn, the president took this to be a personal spiritual message from the American statesman Daniel Webster, whose portrait hung on the wall.

Face of death
Lincoln also apparently saw what some might believe to be his own spirit. He told journalist Noah Brooks that one day, not long before he was elected president, he lay down exhausted on a sofa and was taken aback by what he saw in a mirror opposite him. The glass reflected a double image of himself: one face was normal, but the other was deathly pale, like that of a corpse. Several days later he saw the same thing. Although he explained it away to others as simply an optical illusion, it may have been a hallucination produced by a subconscious fear. Lincoln's wife was certainly anxious for his safety, and feared that the strange reflection was a portent of his death in office.

The haunted restaurant
Houses, castles, prisons, theaters, cinemas, factories, colleges, stores, stadiums — almost every type of structure built for human occupation has provided some stories of ghosts. Restaurants are no exception, and in America there are a number that are said to be haunted.

According to Arthur Myers's book *The Ghostly Register* (1986), one such is Ashley's Restaurant, a mock-Tudor building dating from the late 1920's, on South U.S. Route 1, Rockledge, Florida. Waitresses and bartenders working there have reported that glasses and dishes often fall to the ground on their own; Judi Cowles, manager of the restaurant from 1979 to 1984, claims that customers have reported being pushed by an unseen presence; and the police have reports of burglar alarms going off with no sign of a break-in, and of lights switching on when the building is empty.

Several ghosts have also reportedly been spotted in various parts of the restaurant,

Grace Coolidge
The wife of President Calvin Coolidge was the first person to claim to have seen the ghostly figure of Abraham Lincoln.

Winston Churchill
The great British statesman was one of several eminent witnesses who have been reported as seeing the ghost of Lincoln in the White House.

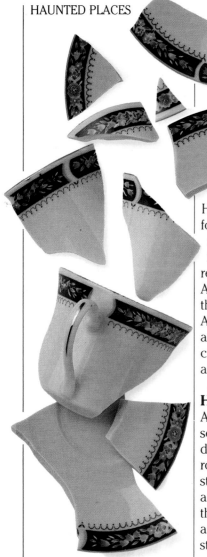

but the main focus of the haunting is said to be the ladies' room. For this room is supposedly frequently visited by the spirit of a young woman, Ethel Allen, who was murdered in the 1930's. Her mutilated and burned body was found at Eau Gallie, on the banks of the nearby Indian River, but the last place in which she was seen alive was the restaurant. On a visit to the restaurant, American psychic Jean Stevens claims that she saw, while in a trance, Ethel Allen's murder taking place. A man with a knife chased the girl downstairs, caught her near the front of the building, and stabbed her to death.

High-button boots
A number of women have reported seeing the image of a young woman dressed in 1920's style in the ladies' room mirror. And Judi Cowles tells of a strange experience she had one night after the restaurant closed. She was in the ladies' room when she noticed, in an adjoining toilet, a pair of feet in 1920's-style high-button boots. When she emerged, the other toilet was empty — though she had heard no one leaving.

"I think," Jean Stevens says, "some places...attract this kind of activity. The land this building is on is one of them."

Musical spirit
Also recorded in Myers's book, *The Ghostly Register*, is the story of another female ghost — in this case, a musical one — which is said to haunt the music department in Knight Hall, part of Pacific University, at Forest Grove, Oregon. It is claimed that the ghost, known to faculty members and students by the name of Vera, sings and plays the piano.

One Christmas Day in the early 1980's, Dr. Donald Schwejda, then a professor of music at the university, wanted to record some music. Because there was too much noise at home, he decided to tape the music at Knight Hall, which was deserted during the vacation. He says he was in the middle of recording when he heard footsteps in the hall outside.

POLTERGEISTS
Inexplicable activity, such as lights turning on and off by themselves and the smashing of crockery, is usually explained as being caused by a poltergeist. This word comes from the German for "noisy spirit." However, phenomena associated with poltergeist activity include far more than inexplicable noises. Poltergeist events allegedly include spontaneous fires, flooding without any water source, and bombardment by objects.

Focus of activity
Research suggests that poltergeist occurrences may be linked to certain individuals, often children, who become the focus of this kind of activity. It is thought that their minds are involuntarily causing these weird happenings. This phenomenon is called recurrent spontaneous psychokinesis (RSPK).

Worried that someone was about to enter and spoil the tape, he tiptoed across the room and opened the door — only to find that the hall was empty.

Blue light
A graduate of Pacific University claims that one night in the 1960's, when he was a part-time watchman in the building, he heard a female voice singing in Knight Hall. When he investigated, he found the building was empty. Even so, he reports, the singing continued and, as he was about to leave, he saw in the hall a blue light in the shape of a woman.

In 1979 two reporters on the student newspaper *Pacific Index* claimed to have spent an unnerving night in the building. They heard footsteps, a woman singing, and the rustling of material. When one of the students began playing the piano, he apparently heard the voice of a woman whispering in his ear, "Oh, please stop!"

Knight Hall
A musical ghost is reputed to haunt this university building at Forest Grove, Oregon.

Rumor has it that the alleged ghost is a music student who either committed suicide or died by accident while working in the building. Kenneth Combs, former music professor and director of planning at the university, says that the ghost was named following a ouija board séance held by an English professor and some students. According to Combs, the spirit was contacted and the board proceeded to spell out the name Vera. Research revealed that there had once been a music student at the department called Vera, who had died young. "I'm not sure she committed suicide," says Combs, "It's said she died in the building, but that could just be a story."

CASTLE GRANT

Historic castles in Britain are considered somehow lacking unless they contain their own resident ghosts. Castle Grant in the highlands of Scotland lays claim to several such spirits.

WHEN LADY BARBARA GRANT of Castle Grant, near Grantown-on-Spey in Grampian, Scotland, was ordered by her father, a ruthless 16th-century chieftain, to marry a man from another clan whom she did not love, she refused to obey him.

In *A History of Clan Grant* (1983), Lord Strathspey, a descendant of the Grant family, described what happened next. In a tapestry room at the top of one of the castle towers, "there was a hidden door leading into a 'blackness' into which Lady Barbara was thrust until she obeyed her father's wishes." Legend has it that she did not obey him, but chose instead to starve to death. Ever since, her ghost has apparently returned to haunt the tower, which was named Babett's Tower in her memory.

Macabre relic

Originally known as Ballachastell, Castle Grant is an imposing structure that has been greatly enlarged and altered over the past five centuries. Originally, it was the stronghold of another clan, the Comyns, whose last leader was killed by a Grant known as Hard Ian.

It is said that the last Comyn's skull was cut into two halves, hinged, and kept as a lucky charm by the Grants. Lord Strathspey, who recalled seeing it as a young boy at Castle Grant, wrote: "There is supposed to be a kind of legendary curse on this relic, that if it passes out of the possession of the family, then the family would lose all its property in Strathspey." Apparently, it is still closely guarded today.

Such family stories, passed down from generation to generation, have undoubtedly been embellished over the centuries. However, they usually originate in historical fact, and more often than not, illustrate the bloody history of the Grant clan.

The Grant family also claims that a phantom piper may be heard playing plaintive tunes around the walls of the castle. Another haunting has been reported at Cullen House, a second Grant stronghold about 40 miles away. Here, in the 18th century, the deranged 3rd earl of Seafield murdered his land agent, then committed suicide, only to reappear, it is said, in spirit form. Over 200 years later, his distraught pacing so distressed the late countess of Seafield that she had his ghost professionally exorcised.

"Trace" ghost

More recently, in 1984, the English photographer Simon Marsden visited Castle Grant and met a workman there, who informed him that he had never seen any of the legendary ghosts. What the workman had seen, on several occasions and in broad daylight, was the figure of a serving maid, passing dishes to someone unseen in the old dining room.

The workman had his own theory about this specter. He said it was what is known as a "trace" spirit, which he described as a ghost that performs an action that was habitual in life.

The ghost of the serving maid lacks the drama of Lady Barbara and does not yet feature in the annals of the Grant clan. Its very mundaneness, however, might be more convincing to skeptics.

> In a tapestry room at the top of one of the castle towers, "there was a hidden door leading into a 'blackness' into which Lady Barbara was thrust."

Death in the tower
The imposing entrance to Castle Grant. On the left is Babett's Tower, where the defiant Lady Barbara is said to have starved to death.

"With ensigns displayed, drums beating, muskets going off, cannons discharged, horses neighing... pell-mell to it they went."

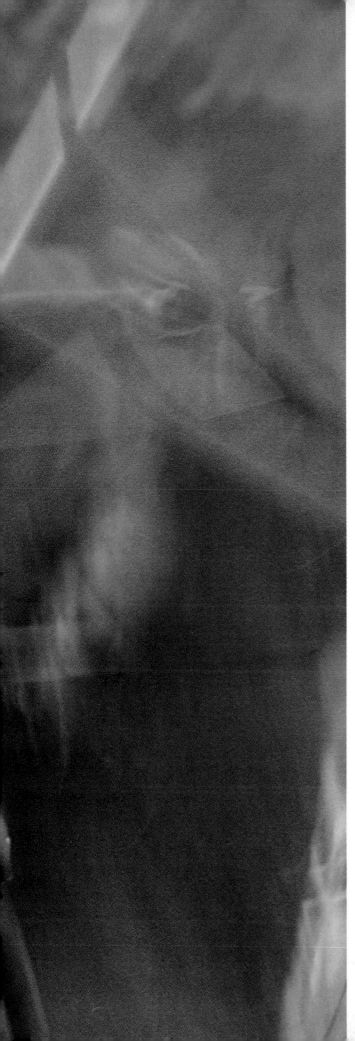

Armies of the Night

On battlefield sites in many parts of the world, phantom troops have apparently been sighted during the hours of darkness, reenacting their bloody conflicts.

ETWEEN MIDNIGHT AND ONE O'CLOCK one Saturday night in 1642 shortly before Christmas, an awestruck group of shepherds, other country people, and travelers reportedly watched at Edge Hill, in England, a ghostly reenactment of an English Civil War battle that had been fought on that spot two months earlier.

The war, which began earlier that year, was a struggle for supremacy between King Charles I and Parliament, a conflict that was to result in the king losing not only his crown but his head. The Battle of Edgehill, fought on October 23, 1642, was the first real conflict of the war. The army of the Royalists (also known as Cavaliers), led by King Charles's nephew Prince Rupert, was evenly matched with that of the Parliamentarians (or Roundheads), under the Earl of Essex, and the action, bloody and confused, was inconclusive, with both sides claiming victory.

Soldiers' groans

Now, on this December night, it seemed that phantoms were fighting the battle all over again. This, at any rate, is the story told in a pamphlet published in London in January 1643: "A Great Wonder in Heaven Shewing The Late Apparitions and prodigious noyes of War and Battels, seen on Edge-Hill." According to this account, the witnesses' first intimation of the "battle" was the sound of distant drums. This was followed by "the noise of soldiers...giving out their last groans." Next came a visual reenactment of the conflict: "With ensigns displayed, drums beating, muskets going off, cannons discharged, horses neighing...pell-mell to it they went."

Rooted to the spot

The battle supposedly lasted about three hours. Those watching were rooted to the spot — mainly because, according to the pamphlet, "run away they durst not, for fear of being made a prey to these infernal soldiers...." When the tumult had finally subsided and the phantom troops vanished from view, the onlookers raced to the nearby town of Kineton and found the local magistrate, William Wood. At first, Wood thought his excited callers were mad or drunk, but, since he knew that some of them at least were "of approved integrity" and since they swore upon oath that their

> # Half an hour later there "appeared in the same tumultuous warlike manner the same two adverse armies, fighting with as much spite and spleen as formerly."

story was true, he called in his neighbor, Samuel Marshall, the minister.

Wood and Marshall agreed to visit the site themselves the following night to see if the ghostly armies reappeared. By the time they set off, the story had spread through the locality, and "all the substantial men of that, and the neighboring parishes grew thither." Half an hour later, so the story goes, there again "appeared in the same tumultuous warlike manner the same two adverse armies, fighting with as much spite and spleen as formerly." The crowd fled, "terrified with these visions of horror...beseeching God to defend them

Sightings recorded
Witnesses' accounts of the phantom Battle of Edgehill were set down in this pamphlet in 1643.

from these hellish and prodigious enemies."

Wood sent men to watch on the following nights, but they saw and heard nothing. It seemed that the haunting was at an end. Then, on the Saturday night following the first sighting, witnesses claimed, the phantom armies clashed again, "with far greater tumult...for four hours... and then vanished."

Wood and many other townsmen could take no more. They "forsook their habitations...and retired themselves to more secure dwellings." Samuel Marshall, the minister, was made of sterner stuff, however, and he stayed on to see further reenactments of the conflict the following weekend. He then traveled to Oxford to inform the king of the amazing and terrifying sightings.

"Sweating in their beds"

Another pamphlet, "The New Yeares Wonder," published a few days after the first, tells of some inhabitants of Kineton being awakened one January night by "the dolfull and hydious groanes of dying men" and the noise of drums and trumpets, "as if an enimye had entred in their towne to put them to a sudaine exicution and plunder all their estates." Some local townspeople confessed to lying "sweating and halfe smothered in their beds," fearing imminent death. Those brave enough to look out of their windows saw "armed horsemen riding one againe the other and so vanisht all."

Bloody battle
This 1870's history book illustration, taken from an engraving, shows armed horsemen fighting to the death for the royal standard at the Battle of Edgehill.

On hearing Samuel Marshall's story, the king dispatched a royal commission to investigate. Led by Col. Lewis Kirke, it consisted of two other officers and three high-ranking civilians. The commission, which arrived in the third week of January, inspected the battlefield and questioned a number of witnesses.

Then, so they reported, on the Saturday and Sunday nights after their arrival, they themselves "heard and saw the prodigies." They swore upon their oath to the king that among the various apparitions they had recognized was the ghost of the Knight Marshal, Sir Edmund Verney, who had valiantly carried the royal standard into battle before being struck down dead by a Roundhead sword.

Mysterious urge

Down the centuries there have been repeated reports of the battle being reenacted in spectral form. In his history of the campaign, *Edgehill 1642* (1967), Brigadier Peter Young describes the strange experience of an English concert pianist, Michaeli. The musician, who had experienced a mysterious urge to visit the site since he was a child, eventually did so with two friends in June 1960. As they drove through the countryside, Michaeli began to realize that all the scenery was familiar to him, even though he had never visited the area before. Even more disturbing was the agitation he felt when they approached a spot where Cavaliers and Roundheads had been buried: he was convinced that hundreds of unseen men were watching him.

Haunted by a Roundhead

More alarming still, so the pianist claimed, was that he returned to his London house and found himself haunted for a month by a Roundhead ghost, dressed in armor and with a piercing gaze. Michaeli sensed that the

Harriet Martineau
The 19th-century historian wrote of ghostly troops sighted in the Lake District.

spirit was hostile to him, and said he had to keep all his lights on at night. He described the experience as the most terrifying and memorable of his life.

Mass hysteria?

How are we to explain all these sightings of phantom troops? Could the reenacted battles reportedly seen by the inhabitants of Kineton have simply been the result of mass hysteria? Those in a state of heightened suggestibility, as the townspeople undoubtedly were, do not make the most convincing of witnesses. Yet on the other hand, this theory does not explain the original sighting. And the pianist Michaeli was certainly no hysteric; as he himself pointed out, his profession taught and demanded extreme emotional control.

The pamphlet "A Great Wonder in Heaven" concluded: "What this doth portend...time perhaps will discover...." But, as with most alleged hauntings, it is unlikely that the passage of time will reveal the truth about the phantom battle that so many people believed they had witnessed.

Fell force

Spectral troops, this time unidentified, were seen in another part of England during the following century. According to the English historian and political commentator Harriet Martineau (1802–76), in her book *Guide to the English Lakes* (1876), the apparitions were seen periodically on Souther Fell, a hill in the scenic area of the Lake District.

The first alleged sighting took place on June 23 (Midsummer Eve), 1735. A farm servant of Mr. Lancaster, a local

Deceptive tranquillity
On this peaceful hill in Cumbria, England, many witnesses once claimed to have seen a phantom army on the march.

▶ PAGE 55

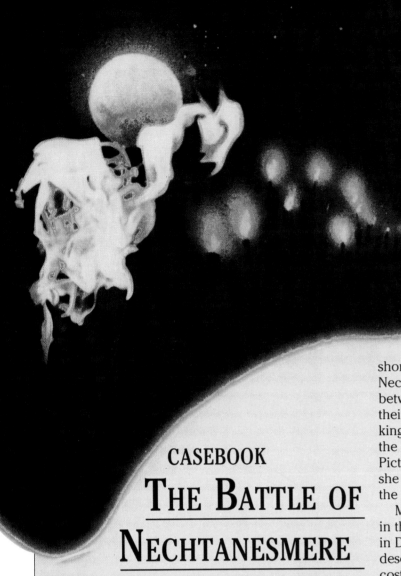

CASEBOOK
THE BATTLE OF NECHTANESMERE

One night in Scotland, on the site of an ancient battle, a woman saw the ghosts of the victors burying their dead comrades.

On JANUARY 2, 1950, a middle-aged woman (identified in this account as Miss S.) was returning from an evening meal with friends to the Scottish village of Letham. Unfortunately, her car skidded into a ditch, and she set out on the eight-mile walk home, in the dark, with only her dog for company.

Nearing home at about 2 A.M., she reportedly saw a strange sight in the desolate countryside. According to her account, she saw: "people who looked as if they were carrying flaming torches....They looked as if they were in...dark tights...a sort of overall, with a roll collar....The one I was watching...would bend down and turn a body over and, if he didn't like the look of it, he just turned it back on its face and went on to the next

one....I supposed they were going to bury them." The field where Miss S. saw these figures is the site of an ancient loch, now disappeared. Around the shores of this loch, in A.D. 685, was fought the Battle of Nechtanesmere. It was a particularly bloody contest between the Northumbrians, under the command of their king, Ecgfrith, and the Picts, commanded by their king, Brude mac Beli. On Saturday, May 20 of that year, the invading Northumbrians were ambushed by the Picts and massacred. Miss S. was convinced that what she saw, more than 1,200 years after the event, was the Picts burying their dead the night after the battle.

Miss S.'s account was recorded by James F. McHarg in the British Society for Psychical Research's *Journal* in December 1978. He pointed out that Miss S.'s description of the site of the battle and of the Picts' costume was consistent with the data available from contemporary sources. McHarg also wrote that Miss S. said that, at the time of the sighting, she was aware that an important battle had taken place near her village, but knew none of the details.

Skirting the loch
Two years before the sighting, in 1948, the historian Dr. F. T. Wainwright, of Queen's College, Dundee, had published an article in the magazine *Antiquity* about the actual site of the loch. According to his research, its shape would have included a projection to the northeast, not immediately obvious from the contours of the land. In her account of the ghostly figures, Miss S. referred to this projection of the now nonexistent loch (or "mere"). She said that the figures were "obviously skirting the mere, because they didn't walk...straight across to the far corner of the field, they came round."

Miss S. claimed not to have read Dr. Wainwright's article. If this is true, the accuracy of her account becomes more beguiling. How could she have correctly located the battlefield around the shores of the now-vanished loch — unless, of course, the mysterious figures she saw that night really were the ghosts of the ancient Pictish warriors?

landowner, claimed that on that evening he watched a body of troops emerge from a niche on the north side of the fell's summit and march about on the east side for approximately an hour before vanishing. "When the poor fellow told his tale," recorded Miss Martineau, "he was insulted on all hands, as original observers usually are when they see anything wonderful."

Mocker mocked

One of the servant's tormentors was Mr. Lancaster, his employer. But ironically, Lancaster himself was to become the object of local ridicule. For two years later he, too, claimed to have seen the spectral force. It was on the same evening of the year that the first sighting had occurred — Midsummer Eve. Lancaster and his family were riding by the base of the fell when, Lancaster alleged, they beheld "an interminable array of troops, five abreast, marching from the eminence and over the cleft as before. All the family saw this, and the manoeuvres of the force, as each company was kept in order by a mounted officer, who galloped this way and that." Following the incident, Martineau reported, Lancaster kept watch on the fell and satisfied himself that the ghostly troops appeared on Midsummer Eve each year.

Sober witnesses

In 1745, again on Midsummer Eve, 26 witnesses, carefully chosen for their sobriety, went with Lancaster to Souther Fell. There, they claimed, they too saw the marching army, this time accompanied by horse-drawn carriages. "There was nothing vaporous or indistinct about the appearance of these spectres," wrote Martineau. "So real did they seem that some... went up the next morning to look for the hoofmarks...and awful it was to them to find not one footprint on heather or grass."

> **"So real did they [the specters] seem that some...went up the next morning to look for the hoofmarks...."**

But of what actual military troops were these phantoms supposed to be the spirits? No known battle was ever fought on or near that site, and, even for those who believed in the apparitions, the visitation remained a mystery.

Marathon rerun

Accounts of dead soldiers' spirits haunting the battlefield where they were slain date back to ancient times. The Greek geographer Pausanias (*fl.* A.D. 143–176) recorded one such story in his *Description of Greece*. In the year 490 B.C. the Athenians had defeated a superior Persian force at Marathon in Greece. More than 600 years later, wrote Pausanias, people living around the plain of Marathon would hear, night after night, in the vicinity of the dead troops' burial mounds, the sounds of the battle being reenacted.

Battle in the sky
In June 1815 the inhabitants of Verviers, a Belgian town about 65 miles west of Waterloo, claimed to have seen phantom troops enacting the Battle of Waterloo (which took place that month) in the sky above the town. This illustration of the phenomenon appeared in a French scientific volume of the late 19th century.

Greek drama
This Greek vase painting depicts a Greek soldier engaging his Persian foe at the Battle of Marathon.

THE HAUNTED HOUSE

"I saw the figure of a tall lady dressed in black, standing at the head of the stairs. After a few minutes she descended the stairs and I followed...."

THESE ARE THE WORDS Rosina Despard, a young Englishwoman, wrote in the journal she kept from 1882 to 1884. She was describing her first sight of the apparition that from then on, so she said, was to haunt the house in Cheltenham, England, in which she lived. Rosina was no hysterical Victorian miss, overfed on Gothic romances. On the contrary, she was a serious-minded, intelligent woman who soon afterward was to graduate with honors in medicine — a rare achievement for a woman in those days.

Fascinated by the apparition, Rosina chronicled its appearances and also researched the history of the house. A few years later her account was published by the Society for Psychical Research, a British organization dedicated to investigating psychic phenomena and reports of paranormal happenings.

Violent arguments

The house, a manor known then as Garden Reach, still stands today on Pittville Circus Road. Renamed St. Anne's, it is now an imposing building converted into apartments. Built in 1860, it was bought that same year by an affluent gentleman, Henry Swinhoe, who moved in with his wife. After his wife died, Swinhoe remarried, and both he and his second wife, Imogen, began drinking heavily. By the early 1870's both were alcoholics, given to violent, drunken arguments.

Apparently, the main point of dispute was the first Mrs. Swinhoe's jewels. Imogen thought that she should have them, but Henry wanted to keep them for the children of his first marriage and hid them under the floorboards in a front sitting-room.

Never frightened

A few months before Swinhoe's death on July 14, 1876, Imogen left him and went to live in Clifton, on the outskirts of Bristol. Two years later, on September 23, 1878, she herself died, and her remains were brought back to Cheltenham to be interred in a churchyard close to the house in which she had lived so unhappily.

After Swinhoe's death, Garden Reach passed briefly into new ownership, and then, after remaining empty for four years, it was rented in April 1882 to Rosina Despard's father, Captain F. W. Despard. He moved in with his wife, four daughters, two sons, and a retinue of servants. At that time Rosina was 19 years old.

In was in June 1882, after she had retired to her room for the night, that Rosina Despard saw the ghost for the first time. She managed to follow it for a short

Frederic W. H. Myers
Myers was a pioneer in the field of parapsychology and a founder-member of the British Society for Psychical Research. He was impressed with the substantial journal of hauntings that Rosina Despard sent him.

St. Anne's, Cheltenham
Formerly Garden Reach, the haunted house still stands today on Pittville Circus Road.

distance, but suddenly her candle went out, and she was forced to grope her way back to her room in darkness.

Even though she quickly suspected the mysterious female to be a ghost, Rosina claimed that she was never frightened of her. The description she entered in her journal is remarkably detailed and precise: "A tall lady dressed in black of a soft woollen material.... The face was hidden in a handkerchief held in the right hand....I saw the upper part of the left side of her forehead, and a little of the hair above. Her left hand was nearly hidden by her sleeve...a portion of a widow's cuff was visible on both wrists, so that the whole impression was of a lady in widow's weeds. There was no cap on the head, but a general effect of blackness suggests a bonnet, with long veil, or a hood."

Passed through tripwire
The ghost was quite solid looking, claimed Rosina, and was liable to appear at any time. Usually, it remained for only a few moments, but once the girl was able to observe it carefully for half an hour. Interestingly, according to Rosina, the specter appeared to know that it was being watched. On two occasions, the young woman reported, she laid a tripwire of thread just beyond the stairs, and watched as the ghostly figure passed right through it.

"A sort of gasp"
"I also attempted to touch her, but she always eluded me," Rosina wrote. "It was not that there was nothing to touch, but that she always seemed to be beyond me, and if followed into a corner, simply disappeared." The girl claimed that she also tried to speak to the ghost, but its only response was "a sort of gasp." Rosina wrote that footsteps were heard by both herself and other members of the household. On January 31, 1884, she wrote: "Her footstep is very light, you can hardly hear it, except on the linoleum, and then only like a person walking softly with thin boots."

Investigator impressed
After having seen the dark lady about a dozen times between June 1882 and the summer of 1884, Rosina sent her substantial journal of the hauntings to Frederic Myers, pioneer parapsychologist, critic, essayist, and one of the founder-members of the British Society for Psychical Research. Myers was thrilled by the prospect of observing a haunting firsthand. Beginning May 1, 1886, he visited the Despard household on a number of occasions to interview the inhabitants and take detailed notes.

He was impressed by what he heard. In his preface to Rosina's account of the hauntings (which appeared in 1892, in Volume VIII of *Proceedings* of the Society for Psychical Research, under the pseudonym Miss R. C. Morton), Myers wrote: "The phenomena as seen or heard by all the witnesses were very uniform in character even in the numerous instances where there had been no previous communication between the percipients."

A married sister of Rosina, Mrs. K., claimed to have seen the ghost in the summer of 1882,

a housemaid in the autumn of 1883, and Rosina's nine-year-old brother Willy and his friend in December of the same year. In the summer of 1884 the alleged specter's appearances became frequent.

> **This ghost has been described as a jolly, bearded fisherman. His hair is long, in the fashion of the 18th century, and he is dressed in a heavy pullover and seaboots.**

Another of Rosina's sisters reported seeing it in July, and it was said to have appeared at least seven times in the month of August. Even though he never saw the ghost himself, Myers continued to investigate the case, but between 1887 and 1889 the phantom "became much less substantial," according to those who claimed that they saw it. And after 1889 there were no sightings at all.

Failed photography
Myers's investigations revealed that some 10 people in all had claimed to have seen the figure and at least 20 had heard it. Some of them had apparently believed it was a real person. Rosina tried to photograph it, "but on the few occasions I was able to do so, I got no result...at night, a long exposure would be necessary for so dark a figure, and this I could not obtain."

When Rosina Despard was shown a photograph album of the Swinhoe family, she picked out a portrait of one of Imogen's sisters as being most like the figure. Myers, however, declared: "The evidence for the identity of the apparition is inconclusive."

The Despards left Garden Reach in late 1889, and the house was sold to a girls' school. After that, there were no further sightings, but vague rumors persisted that footsteps had been heard. More recently, between 1958 and 1961, three witnesses claimed to have seen the figure of a tall woman dressed in black Victorian dress in another house on Pittville Circus Road, but there have been no further sightings at St. Anne's.

The popular belief is that the phantom was the ghost of Imogen Swinhoe. The story goes that she had asked to be buried in the cemetery down the road so that she could return to search for the jewels she felt were rightfully hers.

Celebrated ghost
Whatever its identity, the Cheltenham Ghost has become justly celebrated in the annals of ghost hunting because of its meticulous chronicling by a sober-minded witness and the favorable impression made by all the witnesses upon a respected investigator. Myers himself described the haunting, in his book *Human Personality* (1903), as "one of the most remarkable and best authenticated on record."

While the ghost of Imogen Swinhoe was a sad, perhaps tragic, figure, the phantom that is supposed to walk the long stone corridor and creaking staircases of the Bridport Arms Hotel in West Bay, England, is entirely different. This ghost has been described by those who claim to have seen it as a jolly, bearded fisherman. His hair is long, in the fashion of the 18th century, and he is said to be dressed in a heavy pullover and seaboots.

The Bridport Arms is a thatched building, dating mainly from the early 15th century, which stands on the seashore close to the harbor. In the 18th century it was a whole terrace, consisting of a small farmstead, two cottages, and an alehouse for seamen. If the ghost is really that of an 18th-century fisherman, the alehouse, with its ancient stone-flagged floor and open fireplace, is where he may have spent many hours during his lifetime.

Cheltenham cemetery
Imogen Swinhoe died in Bristol, but asked to be buried in this cemetery just a quarter of a mile away from her former home.

Phantom fisherman
It was on the ceiling of the Bridport Arms Hotel (below) that this smoky formation appeared (right). It was interpreted by some as an image of the fisherman who apparently haunted the building. Outlined in soot, it was created by smoke from a film-crew's spotlight.

Mr. John Jacobs, the present landlord of the Bridport Arms, says that the specter first appeared during the last century. More recently, during the latter part of the 1980's, two or three guests, a former chambermaid, chef Steve Travers, and his assistant Alison Calder claim to have either seen the ghost or witnessed unusual incidents. By all accounts the ghost is a mischievous, ribald character, given to sexual harassment.

Both the chambermaid and Calder claim to have received the ghost's lusty attentions, feeling ghostly hands on their thighs or hot breath on the back of the neck. In addition, the kitchen staff say they have witnessed literally dozens of telekinetic incidents, such as spoons thrown across the kitchen, gas switches turned on and off, and electric fans suddenly set in motion.

"I started making a list of details and times," says Travers, "but there were so many, I just gave it up. On one occasion, Alison, a visitor, and I stood and watched as all four brass gas taps on one cooking range slowly turned off and then on again. Of course, this sort of thing is normally associated with poltergeist activity, but there's no one here to act as the 'focus' that usually attracts that sort of thing. We're all long past puberty and no more mentally disturbed than any other hotel catering staff."

In addition, Alison Calder recalls how one hotel guest claimed to have seen the ghost of the fisherman — bearded, long-haired, and wearing wet oilskins — in his room. His immediate reaction was to strike out at the "intruder," but apparently his fist went straight through the apparition. "His nerve only really went," remembers Calder, "when he saw that the ghost was actually laughing at him. He demanded that we change his room."

Television debut
The highlight of the ghostly fisherman's career, however, came one day in June 1989, when he became the first phantom to appear, rather obliquely, on television. A British television company, Television South West, was featuring the Bridport Arms Hotel in a series it was planning to run on local ghosts. Called "Favourite Haunts," the show's producer and presenter was David Young, an expert on the folklore of the area.

Everything had gone according to plan, with interviews and filming completed, when a cry of excitement came from one of the cameramen.

Extraordinary image
Outlined in soot on the kitchen ceiling was what he saw as the image of a bearded, long-haired fisherman with dark eyes. "There was no question about how it was formed," said David Young. "The smoke from one of the three spotlights had caused it. What neither I nor the technicians could fathom, was why just one of these identical lamps, all of which were in perfect working order, had caused an image. We tried to reproduce it back at the studio, and couldn't.

"The chances of precisely that image appearing under those circumstances — during a documentary on the ghost — at that location, must be infinitesimal."

THE WHALEY HOUSE

Haunted houses are few and far between, and usually only one ghost is reported. But the Whaley House in California lays claim to no less than four.

History in the haunting
The Whaley House in 1874, not long after it was built. One room was used as the town's courthouse from 1867 to 1871, and some of the hauntings are said to have arisen during this period.

O N OCTOBER 9, 1960, Mrs. Kirby of New Westminster, British Columbia, Canada, was visiting the museum known as the Whaley House in San Diego, California. On entering the old courtroom, she claimed she could see a strange figure, that of a small woman. No one else in the room could see her, but Mrs. Kirby's description was detailed: "She is wearing a long, full skirt, reaching to the floor. The skirt appears to be a calico or gingham, small print. She has a kind of cap on her head, dark hair and eyes, and she is wearing gold hoops in her pierced ears."

Smoke and scent

According to the museum's director, Mrs. June Reading, this is not an uncommon occurrence. She claims that a number of visitors have seen apparitions, heard footsteps and the sound of music, smelled cigar smoke or the fragrance of cologne, and witnessed various telekinetic incidents. Some of them have even photographed these ghostly manifestations (not always successfully) and sent them as evidence of the sightings to the museum's curators.

Built between 1856 and 1857 by Thomas Whaley, a New York businessman who moved to California during the Gold Rush, the Whaley House was the first large home to be constructed in what is now Old Town, San Diego. The museum brochure describes it as "one of the finest examples extant of early Californian buildings."

Four ghosts

According to Mrs. Reading, the house has four resident ghosts. Thomas Whaley, dressed in black frock coat, pants, and black broad-brim felt hat, with cigar in hand, has allegedly been seen by museum curators and visitors. Others have supposedly heard the heavy footsteps of

> **Others have heard the heavy footsteps of the ghost of Yankee Jim Robinson, a drifter who was hanged on the site of the property.... He did not die immediately, but took over 15 minutes to strangle to death.**

the ghost of Yankee Jim Robinson, a drifter who was sentenced to death for attempting to steal a boat. He was hanged on the site of the property before the house was built. By all accounts, he did not die immediately, but took over 15 minutes to strangle to death on the scaffold; today, so popular legend has it, he roams the house seeking revenge for his appalling ordeal.

Child spirit

Many of the alleged telekinetic happenings, such as the moving of utensils and the rocking of chairs in the kitchen, have been attributed to the ghost of Annabelle Washburne, a young friend of one of the Whaley children. It was reported that she ran into a clothesline, and was killed. Thomas Whaley apparently carried her into the kitchen after the accident, and she died there. The other reputed ghost is that of Thomas Whaley's wife. She may have been the figure Mrs. Kirby reported seeing.

The Whaley House sightings pose some interesting questions: Are certain houses more prone to hauntings than others? Or is it the reputation of a dwelling as a "haunted house" that produces reports of seemingly supernatural phenomena?

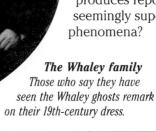

The Whaley family
Those who say they have seen the Whaley ghosts remark on their 19th-century dress.

EXORCISM!

Buildings can be exorcised — and so can people. Many different techniques for the casting out of evil spirits have been developed and practiced by various cultures over the centuries.

Extracting a demon
A 12th-century bronze plaque on the door of the facade of San Zeno church, in Verona, Italy, depicts St. Zeno exorcising a demon out of the mouth of a possessed person.

TECHNICALLY, THE WORD EXORCISM refers to a ceremony used by the Christian Church to expel demons. It comes from the Greek verb *exorkizo* (meaning "to administer an oath" or "to banish an evil spirit") and takes the form of an address to the evil spirits to force them to abandon a place or person.

The rites and practices that primitive people use to ward off or to expel evil spirits belong technically to the field of magic and witchcraft. Nonetheless, their casting-out ceremonies are commonly referred to as exorcisms, and fall into a similar category of experience as the Christian exorcism.

Placating the soul

For centuries exorcisms of one type or another have been performed in allegedly haunted houses. In many parts of the world, primitive man believed that, especially when death occurred suddenly, the mouth of the dead person had to be opened to allow the soul to fly out. The soul often wandered at will and visited places known to it. According to folklore, the first place it haunted was its own dwelling place in life.

Many cultures developed practices to ensure that the soul did not return. In pagan Greece a corpse was buried with a coin in order to pay Charon's fee for ferrying the soul across the mythical river Styx. In India, a corpse's toes were tied together so that the spirit could not reenter the body. And in Europe, the ancient practice of placing a vessel of wine and water and a cake on the place where the body had lain was believed to propitiate or placate the soul. If this practice was not adhered to, the soul of the departed might wander indefinitely, and exorcism would then be necessary to allow the soul to rest.

Haunted houses and castles

Today, exorcisms are still sometimes practiced. At the famous Borley Rectory, in Essex, England, dubbed "the most haunted house in England," several efforts at exorcism have been attempted. According to Peter Underwood's book *Exorcism!* (1990), between 1863, when the rectory was built, and 1939, when it was burnt down, four successive rectors, their wives, and families saw, heard, and felt inexplicable things — and at one time or another enlisted the help of exorcists to stop these phenomena.

Dangerous demons
Detail from a 16th-century carved chair to be found at the reputedly haunted Chambercome Manor, Ilfracombe, England. It shows two demons in the form of centaurs.

> The soul of the departed might wander indefinitely, and exorcism would then be necessary....

▶ PAGE 64

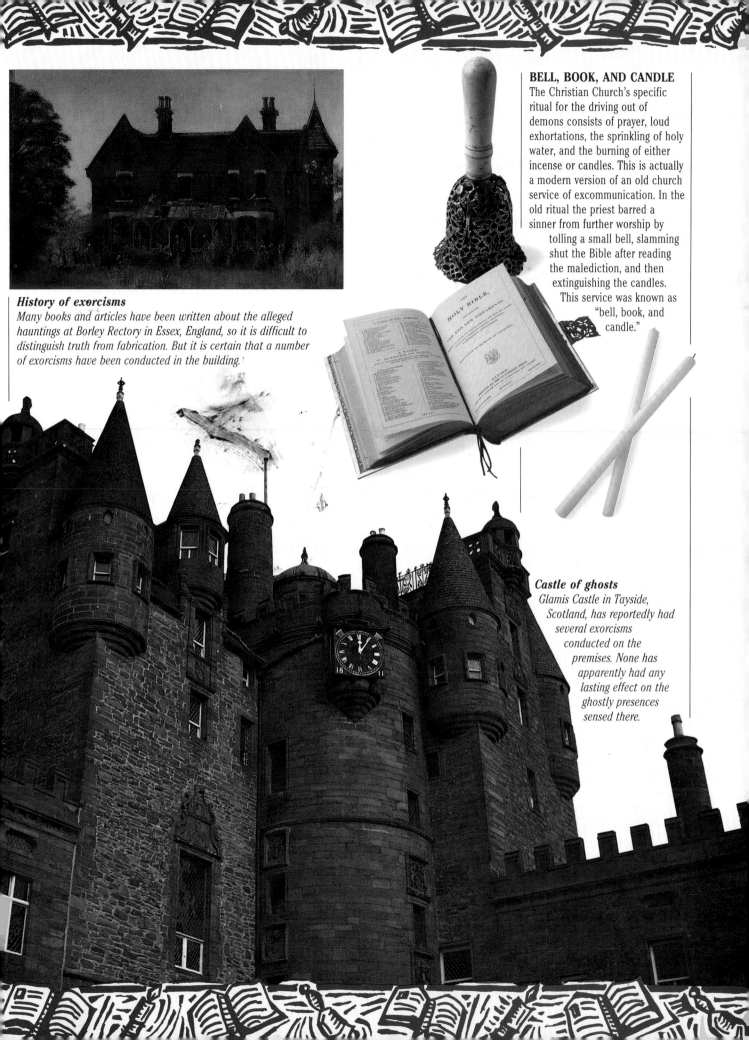

History of exorcisms

Many books and articles have been written about the alleged hauntings at Borley Rectory in Essex, England, so it is difficult to distinguish truth from fabrication. But it is certain that a number of exorcisms have been conducted in the building.

BELL, BOOK, AND CANDLE

The Christian Church's specific ritual for the driving out of demons consists of prayer, loud exhortations, the sprinkling of holy water, and the burning of either incense or candles. This is actually a modern version of an old church service of excommunication. In the old ritual the priest barred a sinner from further worship by tolling a small bell, slamming shut the Bible after reading the malediction, and then extinguishing the candles. This service was known as "bell, book, and candle."

Castle of ghosts

Glamis Castle in Tayside, Scotland, has reportedly had several exorcisms conducted on the premises. None has apparently had any lasting effect on the ghostly presences sensed there.

In March 1931, the Rev. Lionel Foster and two Anglican priests attempted a mild exorcism, sprinkling holy water and scattering incense, but when this had no effect, they performed an elaborate exorcism rite with prayers and exhortations in every room. They followed this procedure with a total fumigation of the house with creosote. Yet, allegedly, the ghosts' activity continued.

According to the author and ghost-hunter James Wentworth Day, reports of exorcisms exist at historic Glamis Castle in Tayside, Scotland. After a visit, Sir Walter Scott (1771–1832) reportedly said: "I began to consider myself as too far from the living and somewhat too near the dead." Yet despite repeated attempts at exorcism by ecclesiastics of various faiths, reports of ghosts at the castle have not ceased.

Exorcism dance drama
The barong *dance drama is performed on the Indonesian island of Bali. The dancers act out a trance state, in which they are possessed by good spirits and perform a ritual battle to exorcise demons.*

Warding off evil
In the Bay of Bengal region of India and Bangladesh, there is a tradition of placing carved wooden figures, such as the one below, above doorways to prevent evil from entering a house.

Exorcising people

People can be exorcised as well as buildings. According to ancient Christian belief, an evil spirit who has possessed a person must be requested to leave through the process of exorcism. Although not every religious community today accepts this view, some more traditional groups do. For example, the Catholic Church and the Hasidic sect of Orthodox Jews believe in possession by spirits, and retain rites of exorcism. Various groups of the Pentecostal movement among North American Protestants frequently perform exorcisms.

Methods of exorcism

In the Bible, Jesus is described as expelling demons with a word. The early Christian Church devised a number of methods to remove evil spirits from possessed persons. By about A.D. 250, there appeared a special class of lower clergy called exorcists, and they were given the function of casting out demons.

In primitive cultures, shamans or witch doctors are the counterparts of Christian exorcists. When evil is said to enter a house, the shaman will be consulted and asked to chant a blessing or cast a spell to drive out the evil spirit. Fetishes (images or other objects believed to have magic power) are placed above doorways of houses or in strategic places to ward off evil spirits, and dance is often used as a medium in the expulsion of demons.

In modern times, demonic possession is most often explained in terms of mental disorder. People who report hearing voices are often diagnosed as suffering from schizophrenia or mental breakdown. This type of medical, or scientific, explanation is attractive to those who are skeptical about the paranormal.

> An evil spirit who has possessed a person must be requested to leave through the process of exorcism.

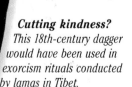

Cutting kindness?
This 18th-century dagger would have been used in exorcism rituals conducted by lamas in Tibet.

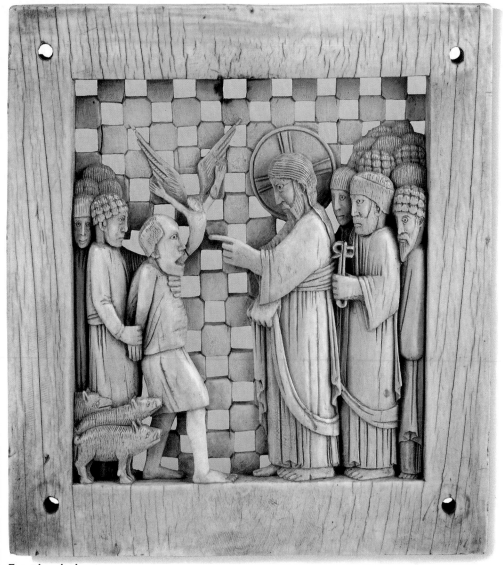

Exorcism in ivory
A 12th-century ivory carving from Italy shows Christ exorcising a demon from a possessed person. It was commonly believed that demons entered and left the body via the mouth.

EXORCISM AT BIRTH

During the Reformation in the 16th century, the Anglican Church published many new tracts and guidelines for its priests. The following baptism service was published in the *First Prayer-Book of Edward VI:*

"Then let the priest, looking upon the children, say: 'I command thee, unclean spirit, in the name of the Father, of the Son, and of the Holy Ghost, that thou come out, and depart from these infants, whom our Lord Jesus Christ has vouchsafed to call to His holy baptism, to be made members of His body and of His holy congregation. Therefore, thou cursed spirit, remember thy sentence, remember thy judgment, remember the day to be at hand wherein thou shalt burn in fire everlasting prepared for thee and thy angels. And presume not hereafter to exercise any tyranny toward these infants whom Christ hath bought with His precious blood, and by this His holy baptism calleth to be of His flock.'"

Demonic implications

Because it was later deemed uncharitable to imagine that all who came to baptism were possessed by demons, it was thought prudent by reformers to omit the words above in later revisions of the liturgy.

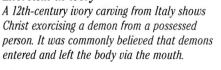

Magical diviner
This traditional Zulu diviner from South Africa is holding a fetish. She is the first person local people turn to when they want to remove evil from sick or possessed persons.

HOUSE OF HORROR?

The most notorious "haunted house" in the world has to be the DeFeo house at 112 Ocean Avenue, Amityville, Long Island. It overshadows other haunted house tales — and its association with violence and horror is a very real one.

THE HORROR BEGAN in the early morning of November 13, 1974, when 24-year-old Ronald DeFeo ran screaming into a bar near his home. Someone, he sobbed, had broken into the DeFeo house and slaughtered his family. The police found his mother, father, two sisters, and two brothers shot dead as they lay in their beds. But the story of an intruder was never believed and Ronald DeFeo was brought to trial charged with the crimes. The prosecution described the motive as a wild attempt to lay hands on $200,000 worth of life insurance, and, finally, DeFeo was sentenced to six consecutive life terms in prison.

Bargain price

After the trial, the imposing three-story Dutch colonial house went on the market at the bargain price of $80,000. Even so, it stayed empty for over a year until, on December 18, 1975, the Lutz family moved in.

> **Kathy Lutz claimed that invisible arms embraced her and tried to gain possession of her body. "Escape was impossible and she felt she was going to die."**

George Lutz, aged 28, was the owner of a land-surveying company. The rambling house seemed ideal for him and his wife, Kathy, and their two young sons and five-year-old daughter. Yet the Lutzes fled 112 Ocean Avenue after 28 days — victims, so they said later, of a relentless, nameless terror.

The full story of their ordeal appeared in the book, *The Amityville Horror* (1977). Written by a reporter, Jay Anson, but based on many interviews with the Lutzes themselves, the book soon became a bestseller.

According to this account, the alleged "haunting" began in dramatic fashion: the house became filled with overpoweringly foul stenches. At the same time, the bathroom porcelain turned dark, stained with a black slime that resisted all household cleaners. Then came the flies — hundreds

of them swarming into a second-floor bedroom. Within days the garage door was wrenched out of its frame, a feat said to "require a strength far beyond that of any human being." This time, though, the culprit had left tracks in the snow. They were reportedly the tracks of cloven hooves, and at last the Lutzes realized that their dream-house was haunted by malignant presences.

Kathy Lutz was the first to be truly terrorized by the frightening entities. She claimed that invisible arms embraced her and tried to gain possession of her body. "Escape was impossible and she felt she was going to die," wrote Anson. It was not only the family who were affected. A priest who befriended them went down with an infection that defied all diagnosis.

At Ocean Avenue, George Lutz reportedly

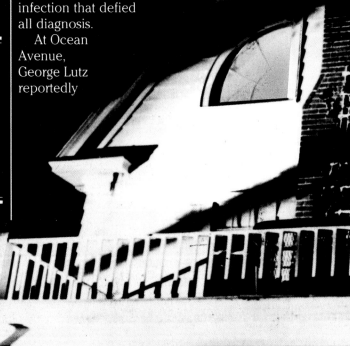

began to experience his own private horror – the sound of a marching band parading around the house, boots thumping and horns blaring. Kathy developed hideously painful red weals on her body. It looked as if a red-hot poker had singed her skin, but the Lutzes claimed that they were the result of "the entity" indulging in sadistic play.

It should all have ended after the Lutzes made a dramatic exit from 112 Ocean Avenue on January 14, 1976. Yet, according to the sequels, *The Amityville Horror – Part II* and *Part III*, written by John G. Jones in conjunction with the Lutzes, the evil followed them on to their new homes, even as far as Australia, Asia, and in the skies above the Atlantic. It was apparently a full seven years before deliverance eventually came.

Kathy and George Lutz

An incredibly grim story if true, but it is so like fiction that it prompts the question: Was there ever an authentic horror in the first place? Jerry Solfin of the American Society for Psychical Research visited the house and, in the summer 1978 edition of *Skeptical Inquirer*, wrote: "The case wasn't interesting to us because the reports were confined to subjective responses from the Lutzes, and these were not at all impressive."

The director of the Parapsychology Institute of America, Dr. Stephen Kaplan, concluded: "After several months of extensive research with those who were involved...we found no evidence to support any claim of a 'haunted house.' What we did find is a couple who purchased a house that they economically could not afford. It is our professional opinion that the story of its haunting is mostly fiction."

Damning evidence

A damning report came from investigators Rick Moran and Peter Jordan. They went to Amityville and interviewed various people mentioned in the book. The police rejected the book's claim that they had investigated the house. Father Mancuso (whose real name is Pecorara) flatly denied that he had ever entered the house, and yet the book states that he blessed the place and was ordered out by a phantom voice.

But perhaps the most serious indictment of the story came from Ronald DeFeo's defense lawyer, William Weber, who was also executor of the DeFeo estate and sold the house to the Lutzes. Weber reportedly admitted: "We created this horror story over many bottles of wine....If the public is gullible enough to believe the story, so be it."

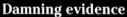

Dark and brooding
The Lutz family moved out of 112 Ocean Avenue (left) after only 28 days, driven out by what they called a nameless terror.

UNRELIABLE MEMOIR
Reexamination of the Amityville case shows that the Lutzes progressively altered their story. At first they spoke only of things felt and sensed, never a word about objective phenomena. But just a year after the alleged haunting, they gave a completely new version of events. This account appeared in the U.S. in the April 1977 issue of *Good Housekeeping* magazine. It clashed with all their previous statements and is in direct conflict with the account given in the Anson book. Although some of the reported events coincide, the contradictions between these two accounts are so great that it is impossible to take them seriously.

Sequel withdrawn
The Lutzes' credibility was further damaged when they had to withdraw their book *The Amityville Horror — Part II*. Later, they were forced to pay damages for libel to the late Dr. Anita Gregory of the British Society for Psychical Research, whose reputation they had smeared in the book.

CHAPTER THREE

GHOSTS WITH A PURPOSE

Ghosts of people that appear to their relatives or loved ones at the moment of death, ghosts that seek forgiveness or offer comfort, and ghosts that warn, admonish, or inform — all appear to be spirits returning to earth with a single purpose.

At about 3:30 A.M. on June 11, 1923, Mrs. Gladys Watson of Indianapolis was awakened by someone calling her name. "I sat up in bed," she claimed afterwards, "and there stood granddad. Very calmly he said, 'Don't be frightened, it's only me. I have just died.'"

According to Mrs. Watson, whose story was reported in the *Journal* of the American Society for Psychical Research, she started to cry when she saw this apparition. But, she recalled, the figure (that of her paternal grandfather) told her

DOUBLE SIGHTING

One day in 1785, when Sir (then Captain) John Sherbrooke and Lieut. George Wynyard were in the latter's sitting room in a regimental barracks in Sydney, Cape Breton Island, Nova Scotia, they were astonished to see a tall, pale young man, about 20 years old, appear in the doorway, then walk through into the bedroom. As related in a biography of Sherbrooke's nephew, *Life and Letters of Viscount Sherbrooke*

Sir John Sherbrooke
Sherbrooke, who between 1816 and 1818 was governor-general of Canada, believed steadfastly in the reality of the apparition he had seen.

(1893), Wynyard recognized the visitor as his brother John, but Sherbrooke did not know him. The two officers followed the figure into the bedroom, where they were astonished to find no trace of him.

In the next mail from England came news that John Wynyard had died there on the same day and at about the same time that the two men had seen him in Nova Scotia.

that he had been "waiting to go" since his wife died. The alleged ghost then disappeared, according to Mrs. Watson.

Mrs. Watson's husband awoke and, upon hearing his wife's story, insisted that she must have had a nightmare — a common enough reaction when someone claims to have seen a ghost. To prove that he was right, Mr. Watson then telephoned the home of his wife's parents, the Reverend and Mrs. Parker, in Wilmington. Mrs. Parker, who took the call, said that she had been up most of the night, because her husband's father had unexpectedly been taken ill and had died at about the time Mrs. Watson claimed to have seen him. The Reverend Parker attributed the experience to the close bond that had always existed between his father and his daughter.

Crisis apparitions

The Gladys Watson case is but one example of what is known in the field of psychical research as a crisis apparition — the ghost of a person appearing, at the time of his or her death, to a loved one or friend. It is presumed they appear to say their last farewells, or to give their relatives due warning of their deaths. Hundreds of examples of such apparitions were collected in *Phantasms of the Living* (1886), the investigative work produced by Edmund Gurney, Frederic Myers, and Frank Podmore for the British Society for Psychical Research.

Myers, in the introduction to the book, comments: "If we can prove that a great number of apparitions coincide with the death of the person seen, we may fairly say...that chance alone cannot explain this coincidence....But if I have a vision of a friend recently dead, and on whom my thoughts have been dwelling, we cannot be sure that this may not be...the mere offspring of my own

brooding sorrow." In *Phantasms of the Living*, the latter type of ghost is called a posthumous apparition, and the former a phantasm of the living, or crisis apparition. A crisis apparition of a dying person is defined as a ghost which appears at any time during a period extending from 12 hours before the person's death to 12 hours after it.

Big grin

In *Extraordinary Experiences* (1989), John Robert Colombo records a case that allegedly occurred in Port Mellon, British Columbia. On May 16, 1985, Mrs. Kathleen Belanger took great pleasure in a Mother's Day visit from her son Roger, his wife Myra, and their two small sons. But after they had left, she claimed, she experienced a strange feeling of dread. In mid-afternoon she arrived home from shopping, she said, and found the garage door, and every door in the basement, wide open. Suddenly, she saw her son Roger standing before her, a big grin on his face. She was about to ask him what was going on, when the figure vanished.

At about 9 o'clock that evening, the police arrived to tell her that Roger had been struck by a falling tree in a logging accident and had died instantly.

Unknown apparition

Reports of crisis apparitions include tales where the alleged ghost that appears is not known by sight to the witness. American psychic investigator and author Brad Steiger relates in his book *True Ghost Stories* (1982), an experience that Mrs. Anna Arrington of New York said occurred when she was a young girl. One day, she had stayed home from school because of a cold, and was just looking out of a window when all of a sudden she saw a strange woman standing next to her. Anna noticed that

> She arrived home from shopping, she said, and found the garage door, and every door in the basement, wide open. Suddenly, she saw her son Roger standing before her, a big grin on his face. She was about to ask him what was going on, when the figure vanished.

she had big brown eyes, and in a letter to parapsychologist Prof. Hans Holzer, she wrote: "She came real close to my face before she vanished. I had never seen her before in my life."

When her father came home, Anna described what she had seen. He immediately recognized the apparition as being that of his Aunt Maggie, and was even more surprised when a telegram arrived at 6 P.M. telling of her death that afternoon.

Suicide case

Sometimes those close to the person whose crisis apparition manifests itself become aware of the apparition only through an intermediary. A case of this kind, concerning a suicide, is cited in *Phantasms of the Living*. At 10 P.M. on November 6, 1868, the wife and daughter of Colonel V. were in their bedroom in Mussoorie, India. Suddenly, the daughter, who was brushing her hair in front of the mirror, exclaimed that she could see Colonel B., a close friend of the family, who lived in Meerut, about 80 miles away. The girl claimed that Colonel B. said: "Goodbye, Sissy — goodbye!" and then disappeared. The room, house, and garden were immediately searched, but there was no sign of Colonel B. Questioned by her father, the girl repeated her story and also described the clothes the figure had been wearing.

Two days later Colonel V. was astonished to read in the press that his friend had shot himself on the day his daughter had reported seeing him. The East India Company confirmed the date of death as November 6, 1868.

Wartime apparitions

During times of war, reports of crisis apparitions increase dramatically. Dr. Charles Richet, professor of physiology at the University of Paris, studied this phenomenon during the First World War. In 1915 he asked French troops to provide him with the details of any paranormal experiences they may have had, along with verification by other independent witnesses if possible.

According to the *Journal* of the American Society for Psychical Research, in its issue of January 1921, Professor Richet received hundreds of letters —

Wartime vision
Reports of apparitions rise during times of war; this First World War song card shows a soldier, far from home, conjuring up a vision of a loved one.

from men of all ranks, differing backgrounds, and levels of education.

One man, Pierre Cotte, wrote: "I had gone to bed and it was about a quarter of an hour after we had said goodnight to each other, my neighbour and I, when I perceived at first an indistinct form leaning on the bar of my bed; this form became clearer and I recognized my foster brother; his voice, which I knew well, said to me: 'How are you, Pierre? As for me, I am going.' I sat up in bed and called my friend; he saw nothing, the form had disappeared."

Four days later, Cotte received a letter from his foster parents informing him of their son's death. He had died on the day that Cotte had seen his ghost.

In another case, a military physician, Dr. Jean,

WAILING SPIRIT

The wailing of the banshee to announce death is a well-known phenomenon in Celtic folklore. Although its name translates as "woman of the fairies," most authorities define the banshee as a spirit rather than a fairy. Indeed, some Irish families regard it almost as a guardian angel, silently watching over family members and directing them in life. When one of them is about to die, the banshee performs her last service — that of mournful "keening" for the soon-to-be departed soul.

Red-haired apparition

Although best known for her distinctive wailing lamentation, the banshee has reputedly appeared as an apparition as well. According to tradition she has long red hair, which she combs as she wails outside the home of the person about to die. However, she is rarely heard or seen by the doomed person.

Harbinger of death
This mid 19th-century book illustration shows the banshee in the form of an old hag, wringing her hands and wailing for the souls of doomed mortals.

wrote to Professor Richet about an experience unconnected with the war. A seven-year-old boy he was attending sat up in bed one morning, crying out that he could see his father drowning. Shortly afterwards, alleged Dr. Jean, the mother received a telegram saying that her husband had died in the sea that morning, while trying to save his brother from drowning.

Form of telepathy

If crisis apparitions are what they appear to be, a fact rather than a figment of the imagination, what might be their cause? A theory, advanced in *Phantasms of the Living*, is that such apparitions might be instances of some form of telepathic communication from the person in crisis to the witness, "the supersensory action of one mind on another." In the case of apparitions occurring shortly after, rather than before, death, the theory suggests that telepathy has been delayed.

Subtle shock

Another theory to explain crisis apparitions was put forward by the French psychical researcher Camille Flammarion in his book *Death and its Mystery* (1922). He suggested that "at the moment of death a subtle shock, unknown in its nature, at times affects those at a distance who are connected with the dying in some way....[This] gives rise to physical phenomena and mental impressions. These emissions are automatic, usually involuntary, and are comparable to electric vibrations which...accompany the sundering of earthly bonds."

Camille Flammarion
The French psychical researcher suggested that apparitions of the dying might be due to a "subtle shock" emanating from the dying person.

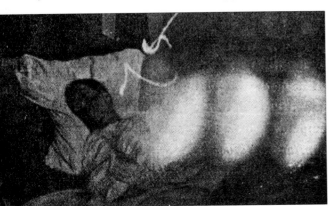

Body and soul?
This photograph, taken shortly after the moment of death, has been advanced as evidence for the spiritualist view that waves of matter or a "soul" leave the physical body when a person dies.

Strong evidence

Some would argue that a crisis apparition has nothing to do with telepathic communication or waves of some kind emanating from a dying person, but is actually the "soul" of a person who has recently died. In the collaborative report "Six Theories about Apparitions" (1956), published in the *Proceedings* of the British Society for Psychical Research, the authors find that the evidence for some form of survival after death is strong. They say that many of the reported crisis apparition cases "have practically perfect authentication ....These well-evidenced cases point toward the reality of such phenomena." And in his later book *The Enigma of Survival* (1959), Prof. Hornell Hart, of Duke University in North

> "Human personality *does* survive bodily death. That is the outcome... when the strongest anti-survivalist arguments and the strongest rebuttals are considered thoroughly, with dispassionate open-mindedness."

Carolina, one of the co-authors of the SPR *Proceedings* report, concludes that: "Human personality *does* survive bodily death. That is the outcome which I find emerging when the strongest anti-survivalist arguments and the strongest rebuttals are considered thoroughly, with dispassionate open-mindedness."

ROLE REVERSAL

In the typical crisis apparition case, a dying person's ghost appears to one or more loved ones. In an unusual instance, however, phantoms of the living family reportedly appeared at the bedside of a dying man.

IN THE FALL OF 1870, during the return voyage of the British steamship *Robert Lowe* from St. Pierre, Newfoundland, one of the ship's engineers, W. H. Pearce, fell ill with typhus. Pearce's close friend, D. Brown, a stoker, volunteered to look after him.

At 3 P.M. on October 3, Brown was attending the sick man. Pearce had become delirious, and Brown was trying to prevent him from getting out of his bunk, when, according to his later testimony, "I saw on the other side of the bunk, the wife, two children, and the mother of the dying man, all of whom I knew....They appeared to be very sorrowful, but in all other respects were the same as ordinary human beings."

Brown noticed that they appeared somewhat paler than usual. However, they were perfectly solid and wearing their ordinary clothes. Pearce himself did not see them, or at least said nothing. Brown then alleged that the mother said in a clearly audible voice: "He will be buried on Thursday, at 12 o'clock, in about fourteen hundred fathoms of water."

The stoker was terrified and rushed out of the berth to the cabin of the captain, J. Blacklock. The captain later reported: "Brown came down...looking very pale and frightened, and declared that he would not attend the sick man any more on any conditions — not for a thousand pounds." Later, other crew members told how they had great trouble soothing the stoker and had only gradually drawn the story of the apparitions from him.

Blacklock characterized the stoker as "a strong, healthy man, not likely to be led astray by imagination."

Detailed statement

It was 16 days later that Captain Blacklock and seven crew members drew up a detailed statement concerning the incident, which was later published in *Phantasms of the Living.* One interesting feature was that the prediction made by the phantom Mrs. Pearce was inaccurate. After he died, Pearce was buried at 4 P.M. on Tuesday, not at midday on Thursday.

There are various theories, all highly speculative, to explain this incident. For example, could the delirious Pearce have summoned up the images of those he loved most in order to bid them farewell? Or might it have been Brown, who knew the family well, who projected a vision of the family from his own mind? The interpretation that believers in crisis apparitions prefer is that Pearce's mother somehow telepathically projected the family across the sea to see her son once more before he died.

A 19th-century print entitled "Burial at Sea"

SEEKING SOLACE

Some ghosts appear to be so guilt-ridden that they wander the earth seeking forgiveness. By contrast, others, apparently at peace, seem to return to offer comfort to the living.

BARON BASIL VON DRIESEN, an inhabitant of Kashin, in Russia, put away the Bible he had been reading in bed and prepared to go to sleep. It was between 1 and 2 o'clock in the morning of November 30, 1860. Later that day a liturgy was to be celebrated for the soul of von Driesen's father-in-law, M. Nicholas Ponomareff, who had died nine days earlier and with whom the baron had not been on good terms.

Shuffling footsteps

In an account published by the British Society for Psychical Research in Volume X of *Phantasms of the Dead* (1894), von Driesen described what happened next: "I had just put out the candle when footsteps were heard in the adjacent room — a sound of slippers shuffling....I called out, 'Who is there?' No answer. I struck one match, then another and...I saw M. Ponomareff standing before the closed door. Yes, it was he, in his blue dressing gown lined with squirrel fur and only half buttoned, so that I could see his white waistcoat and his black trousers.

"I have acted wrongly"

"'What do you want?' I asked my father-in-law. M. Ponomareff made two steps forward, stopped before my bed, and said, 'Basil Feodorovitch, I have acted wrongly towards you. Forgive me! Without this I do not feel at rest there.' He was pointing to the ceiling with his left hand whilst holding out his right to me. I seized this hand, which was long and cold, shook it and answered, 'Nicholas Ivanovitch, God is my witness that I have never had anything against you.'

"[The ghost of] my father-in-law bowed...moved away and went through the opposite door into the billiard-room, where he disappeared. I looked after him for a moment, crossed myself, put out the candle, and fell asleep with the sense of joy which a man who has done his duty must feel."

Double apparition

Von Driesen went on to relate that later that day, after the liturgy had been celebrated, the priest (who also acted as the family's confessor), the Reverend Basil Bajenoff, told the baron and his wife in confidence that the previous night Ponomareff had appeared to him too and begged him to reconcile Ponomareff to his son-in-law. In a written statement on July 23, 1891, Bajenoff

"'I have acted
wrongly
towards you.
Forgive me!'...
I seized this
hand, which was
long and cold,
shook it and
answered...."

confirmed the baron's story with the words: "To me also did he appear *at the same time* and with the same request."

As the authors of *Phantasms of the Dead* said about this case: "The interest lies in the simultaneous appearance [of the ghost] to two percipients who were not together — a coincidence which it is difficult to regard as fortuitous, however it may be explained."

Unredeemed ghosts

In her book *Apparitions and Precognition* (1963), based on letters about paranormal experiences, Aniela Jaffé devotes one section to what she terms unredeemed ghosts, those who can find no rest after death. One woman recalled what happened after her engagement to a young man had been broken off: "Six years later, on a fine summer day...I was busy tidying up the kitchen when suddenly I felt a strange restlessness. What occurred in the next hour is still inexplicable to me, for I did not act according to my conscious will, but under some invisible compulsion."

Deep pity

The woman described how she went to the attic, opened a box containing her former fiancé's letters and began to re-read them. "Suddenly I was overcome by a deep pity for this man...I was sitting there in tears, quite beside myself, when all at once I had the feeling that I was no longer alone in the room. I looked up in fear and before me stood my fiancé....He [said]: 'You must forgive me everything I did to you, I was a poor creature.'

"I stared at him as though hypnotized and said aloud: 'I forgive you everything, you were a poor creature.' When I had finished speaking the figure dissolved into nothingness....Next day I saw the notice of my fiancé's death in the newspaper...he had died the same afternoon when he had compelled me to forgive him everything."

Discussing such reported cases, Jaffé notes that the act of forgiveness seems to bring peace to the souls of both the deceased and the witness: the apparition vanishes and usually makes no further anguished visitations, and the witness ceases to feel grief.

In marked contrast to allegedly restless spirits, troubled by past misdeeds, are those that, according to various claims, are obviously at peace and that appear to offer comfort to the witness. One such case concerns two British theological writers, Canon J. B. Phillips, author of the best-selling *The New Testament in Modern English* (1958), and C. S. Lewis, author of *The Screwtape Letters* (1942) and the *Narnia* books for children.

"One day after his [Lewis's] death," recounted Phillips in *The Ring of Truth* (1967), "while I was watching television, he 'appeared' sitting in a chair within a few feet of me, and spoke a few words which were particularly relevant to the difficult circumstances through which I was passing. He was...positively glowing with health....A week later, this time when I was in bed reading before going to sleep, he appeared again, even more rosily radiant than before, and repeated to me the same message....I mentioned it to a certain saintly Bishop....His reply was, 'My dear J....this sort of thing is happening all the time.'"

Reassuring ghost

In 1970 the British Society for Psychical Research asked Phillips to provide more details of his experience and published this fuller account in its *Journal* of December that year. Phillips revealed that his "difficult circumstances" at the time had been a state of "mental and spiritual depletion" after years of creative work, and that on both occasions when he had seen the ghost of Lewis, it had reassured him with the words: "It's not as difficult as you think, you know."

> The woman described how she went to the attic, opened a box containing her former fiancé's letters and began to re-read them.

Just as comforting, though in a different way, was a ghost reported in Sir Ernest Bennett's *Apparitions and Haunted Houses* (1939). After the death of his wife early on Christmas Day, 1932, Dr.

Healthy ghost?
The celebrated author, C. S. Lewis, was said to be "rosily radiant" when he appeared as a phantom to offer reassurance and comfort to a friend.

Eustace, chairman of the bench of magistrates in Arundel, England, was confident that her spirit lived on and that they would meet again. But gradually he lost this faith and, with a heavy heart, resigned himself to permanent loss.

> "Standing on the lawn beyond the rose garden and thirty yards from me was my wife....Her face and figure were as distinct and clear-cut as in life...."

One evening, at sunset, about seven weeks after his wife's death, Dr. Eustace was walking in his garden, thinking of other matters, when he came to a halt. "Standing on the lawn beyond the rose garden and thirty yards from me was my wife. She stood looking straight at me as though she had been expecting me. Her face and figure were as distinct and

clear-cut as in life...she gazed intently at me...with a puzzled look of remonstrance as though she were surprised and disappointed with me. Translated into words her expression would have been well rendered by: 'How stupid of you! Why so foolish?'....I believe that I smiled and that my face reflected my joy."

Helping hand

Dr. Eustace then learned that a friend of his wife's, Mrs. Welch, had also claimed to have seen the ghost, but much earlier — at a midnight service at the Convent of Poor Clares, in Crossbush, on the eve of Mrs. Eustace's death. According to Mrs. Welch, when she arrived at the service at five minutes before midnight, a figure she recognized as that of Mrs. Eustace took her arm and assisted her to her seat and then to the chancel and back again.

When Mrs. Welch learned the following day of Mrs. Eustace's death, she realized that it was the spirit of her friend that had been at the service and had helped her. Dr. Eustace noted that, standing by his wife's bedside on Christmas Eve, he had observed that she lost consciousness at 11:55 P.M., the exact time that Mrs. Welch claimed to have been helped by her.

Commenting on his own and Mrs. Welch's experiences, Dr. Eustace wrote: "I am well content to leave the interpretation to others, for I know now that I know."

Friendly guidance
It was in this church at the Convent of Poor Clares, Crossbush, England, that an Englishwoman claimed she was assisted to her seat by the spirit of her dead friend.

Missions
and Messages

The aim of some ghosts seems to be to deliver warnings, reproaches, or information. Described here are several dramatic examples of such cases and various theories that might help account for them.

I T WAS TOWARD SUNSET on an evening in October 1932. In the village of Bazsi, Slovenia (formerly part of Yugoslavia), 14-year-old Janos Felker, weary from a backbreaking day in the vineyard gathering late grapes, sat down in a barn and began milking the cows. But, according to Peter Moss, a British writer on the paranormal, who tells the story in a Hungarian book *Találkozott Már Kísértetekkel?* (*Have You Seen a Ghost?*) (1992), Janos was more than weary. He was a boy depressed and ill at ease with himself.

"The wages of sin"
The seventh son of a peasant couple, Janos had been forced to leave school before he was 12 and to work on his uncle's farm, because his family was too poor to support him. The boy's parents were devout and he had been brought up strictly, but in his new life, all that changed. His uncle was not religious and, provided his young charge worked well, Janos was allowed to do whatever he liked. The young men of the village befriended him, and soon he was staying out late with them, drinking, smoking, gambling, and having a good time.

Janos appeared to revel wholeheartedly in his new existence. But deep down he was troubled. He believed he was sinning, and he knew that the Bible proclaims: "The wages of sin is death."

One night, in the barn attic in which he slept, Janos, after a debauched evening with his companions, felt particularly uneasy. As he reflected on the life he was leading, a memory came to him of a schoolmate, Gyula, who had died the previous year, aged only 13. In class Gyula had often, with a whispered warning, enabled Janos to escape the attention of a brutal teacher. Now, with a boy's simple faith, Janos prayed fervently that Gyula would assist him again — this time

to help him to change his ways and to escape a punishment he knew would be far worse than a schoolmaster's beating.

Terrifying knock

Help from Gyula did not arrive, however, and over the following months Janos continued with his existence. One October evening, as he sat milking, he was, in his own eyes, more damned than ever. Suddenly, according to his later account, he heard a terrifyingly loud knock at the end of the barn. He looked up and, although the barn door was closed, saw, standing there in the dim light, a boy holding an old chaff cutter.

> "What the hell do you think you're doing, frightening me like that?... I'll show you what frightening means!"

Assuming it was one of his village friends, he called out angrily: "What the hell do you think you're doing, frightening me like that?" He then turned back to milking the cow.

Sad eyes

The thunderous knock sounded again, according to Janos, and, irritable with fatigue, he shouted: "You bloody idiot, I'll show you what frightening means!" He leaped to his feet and ran toward the boy. As he neared him, he became aware of sad brown eyes fixed on his face. It was not one of the local tearaways — but who it could be he did not know.

With flailing arms, Janos rushed at the boy, but, he claimed, his fists passed right through the figure, which retreated. It seemed to Janos that its eyes were filled with both reproach and pleading. It then appeared to solidify, claimed Janos, but soon faded and seemed to pass through the barn wall. Before it disappeared, however, said Janos, he recognized in the phantom the likeness of his dead friend Gyula. Long after the last outline of the alleged apparition had faded from sight, it seemed to Janos that its accusing, beseeching gaze lingered on in the shadows.

Turning point
Janos Felker was convinced that the phantom he had seen was the ghost of his old friend, come back in answer to his prayer, in an attempt to rescue him from the downward path on which he was set. The experience, Janos claimed, was a turning point in his life. He gave up his old ways, returned to the religion of his youth, and as he grew to manhood became an exemplary citizen.

The question we naturally ask after reading this story is: Was the apparition Janos saw truly the ghost of his childhood friend? Or, fatigued and racked by a guilty conscience as he was, had his own subconscious projected the image of his old friend? Whatever the true nature of the phenomenon, the case is a classic example of the ghost with a mission.

Bargain coat
Another case of a warning ghost, this time an apparition of someone unknown to the witnesses, occurred in Ukraine in the 1890's. The story, documented in the *Proceedings* of the British Society for Psychical Research for 1896–97, concerns Vincent Idanowicz, an engineer, of Creczelowka. On November 10, 1894, Idanowicz visited the nearby town of Gaysin to order a fur coat from a tailor, Izloma Sierota. The tailor showed him an almost new coat, which he said he was selling on behalf of a Mr. Lassota for the cheap price of only 45 rubles. Idanowicz snapped up the offer and returned home with the coat.

Man in black
That night, in the bedroom he shared with his brother Ivan, Vincent Idanowicz saw an unknown man dressed in black.

Saved from sin
After seeing the ghost of an old schoolmate, Janos Felker underwent a radical change of heart. Today he is a man of deep religious faith.

Vincent was not alarmed, he said, only surprised that someone had been able to enter the room, which was locked. According to Idanowicz, the phantom told him: "I am called Wiszniecoski.... Return, as quickly as possible, this fur which you have just bought from Izloma

Was the apparition Janos saw truly the ghost of his childhood friend? Or, fatigued and racked by a guilty conscience as he was, had his own subconscious projected the image?

Sierota for 45 rubles, since it did not belong to Mr. Lassota but to a judge at Gaysin, who has just died of phthisis [tuberculosis]. The fur is infected by phthisic bacilli." The apparition, Idanowicz claimed, then vanished.

Idanowicz ascertained that the locks on the door were indeed secure, and this noise awoke his brother, who, when he heard the story, laughed in disbelief.

Return visit
The following night, the brothers reported, they were talking late in their room when they heard footsteps approaching along the outside passage. They claimed that the door, again double-locked, opened, and the black-garbed stranger appeared again. The phantom allegedly told them that, since they were both awake this time, this would show that he was not a hallucination. He repeated his warning about the infected coat, they said, and urged Vincent to return it the next day. He also told them that he had been a government official who had died two years previously, and that his mission was to watch over Vincent.

The next morning the brothers told their story to their employer and landlord, Joseph de Kronhelm (who wrote the original report on which later accounts of the case were based). Accompanied by Kronhelm, Vincent took the coat to the tailor Sierota, who

▶ PAGE 82

Phantom Footsteps

A dark hospital ward in the early hours of the morning...the sound of ghostly footsteps crossing the corridor...a defenseless baby saved from death....

*I*T WAS A NIGHT IN NOVEMBER 1969. For nurse Pauline Gittins, on duty with two colleagues in the maternity wing of a hospital in Chorley, England, it looked like a routine shift. The babies in the nursery were all well, as were the mothers in the two wards. No births were imminent, and the labor rooms were empty. At about 2 A.M. the nurses finished a tour of inspection and gathered in the kitchen to make some tea.

Flip-flopping sound

Gittins's story of what happened next is recounted in *Ghosts Over Britain* (1977), by Peter Moss. As the three nurses relaxed, they heard the characteristic screech of one of the ward doors opening. They then heard footsteps moving quickly along the corridor past the kitchen door. They made a flip-flopping sound — like that of feet in backless slippers. All three nurses thought that it must be a patient going to the bathroom. But none of them heard the bathroom door opening — an equally distinctive noise.

No one there

Gittins decided to investigate. She found there was no one in the corridor, no one in the bathroom. She next checked the two main wards and saw that all the occupants were fast asleep. Finally, she looked into the labor wards and found them, as expected, empty. Puzzled, she was passing the nursery on her way back to the kitchen when she heard a choking noise. She dashed into the nursery and found a two-day-old baby choking on its vomit, blue from lack of oxygen, and near death. Working swiftly, she managed to clear the infant's air passage. When she was satisfied it was breathing freely again and was completely out of danger, she rejoined her colleagues and described what had happened.

When Gittins had finished her story, one of the other nurses asked who had been walking along the corridor. Only then did the full realization hit Gittins. Whatever the source of the footsteps, she believed, it could not have been a human one. And it also struck her that if the incident had not occurred, she would not have gone out to investigate, and the baby would almost certainly have died.

Projected presence?

If what all three nurses heard on that November night was truly — and it may well not have been — a supernatural message, whose message was it? Was it possible that the baby's mother had sensed, though fast asleep, that her child was in mortal danger, and had somehow projected her presence into the corridor in order to summon help? But if so, why did she appear in a form that could so easily have been ignored or mistaken? Such questions recur constantly: even for those who believe in the existence of ghosts, for whatever reason, the behavior of these phantom beings is sometimes difficult to comprehend.

denied that it had belonged to a dead judge. Kronhelm and Vincent then visited the dead man's successor in the town of Gaysin, who told them that his predecessor had indeed died of tuberculosis and that, as to the dead man's effects, they should consult the second-hand dealer, Boruch Fonkonogi. This dealer stated that he had disposed of all the judge's effects, except the fur coat, which he said he recognized and which he insisted that Sierota had bought.

Story verified

Kronhelm's account of the case was published in June 1895, and over the following months psychical researchers investigated the case in depth, establishing that the story was more or less correct in most of its key details. The fur coat had belonged to Alexander Nevsky, a leading member of the judiciary in Gaysin (though an examining magistrate, not a judge), who on June 28, 1893, had died of tuberculosis.

The government official Wiszniecoski, of whom the alleged apparition in black claimed to be the ghost, was never identified definitely, but a solicitor of the same name was discovered to be living in the nearby town of Il'intsy. When questioned, however, this man knew nothing about Vincent Idanowicz and could provide no further information on the matter.

If the apparition was a true ghost and what it claimed to be — the protector of Vincent Idanowicz — this raises various questions. Why should the spectral "protector" be the spirit of someone with whom the "protected" had no apparent

"Too Late"
This painting by William Windus (1822–1907) epitomizes the despair of a victim of tuberculosis. The scourge of the 19th century, this disease claimed millions of lives.

connection? Did the spirit appoint itself Idanowicz's protector, or was it entrusted with the role by a greater power?

It may have been, of course, as can be postulated for all ghost sightings, that the warning apparition was a purely

> ## "I am called Wiszniecoski....Return, as quickly as possible, this fur which you have just bought from Izloma Sierota for 45 rubles...it belonged to a judge who has just died of tuberculosis."

subjective phenomenon. Idanowicz may have heard at some time that tuberculosis can be contracted from contact with the sufferer's possessions (a risk now known to be minimal) and may, in buying a good-quality coat for such a low price, have worried deep down that there was a good reason for the bargain: the coat was infected.

Unconscious power

It is true that Vincent's brother, too, claimed to have seen the apparition. But, sometimes, in cases of apparition-sightings where there is a close blood relationship between witnesses, it has been suggested, in theory at least, that one member of a family may possess the unconscious power to make other members share his or her hallucinations.

Sometimes the purpose of an alleged ghost's visit is simply to bring news, often of a death in the family, as in this story recounted by its protagonist to Peter Moss, a British writer on the paranormal. One Thursday evening in October 1976, Dr. Anna Peter, a Hungarian barrister, sat in her Budapest apartment trying to improve her German. She was not having much success. She found that, try as she might, she could not concentrate. Her mind kept wandering, and she was restless, getting up constantly to pace about the room and look pointlessly out the window. Finally, giving up the struggle, she went to bed.

"Have you heard?"
At some time after midnight, Dr. Peter was awakened by a voice asking firmly and clearly: "Have you heard?" She instantly recognized the voice as that of her mother, who had died 11 years earlier. Dr. Peter sat up in bed, switched on the light, and saw standing beside her an apparition of her mother, dressed in a bathrobe. The figure was fairly solid and stood erect, not stooping as her mother had in the last year of her life. The phantom leaned forward until its face was within inches of Dr. Peter's and asked again, emphatically: "Have you heard?" Then the apparition vanished.

Question repeated
Dr. Peter, apparently undisturbed by this visitation, switched off the light and fell asleep again. Not long afterward, she said, she heard the same enigmatic question and, switching on the light, again saw her mother. Six more times

---

After midnight, Dr. Peter was awakened by a voice asking firmly and clearly: "Have you heard?" She instantly recognized the voice as that of her mother.

---

that night, she claimed, the phantom spoke again, showing itself on the first two occasions only.

According to Dr. Peter, the next day and night were uneventful, but on the morning of the following day, Saturday, she felt restless again. In the market she felt so distracted that she abandoned her shopping and hurried home.

Sister dead
Dr. Peter described what happened next. As she reached the front door of her apartment, she heard the telephone

ringing. She threw down her shopping basket and rushed in. The caller was her sister Katalin, speaking from her home in Zürich. "Have you heard?" Katalin sobbed, echoing the mysterious query of two days earlier. "Have you heard? Ezster [a third sister, living in Switzerland, who had been ill for some time] died about 9:30 on Thursday evening."

Never close
Afterwards, Dr. Peter asked herself why her mother's apparition had appeared to her, since the two had never been close. Indeed, Anna had lived with her grandparents until she was 10 years old. She could not understand why the message that Ezster was dead had not been communicated to one of her four brothers and sisters, who had all been favored by her mother. It also seemed strange to Dr. Peter that the message that Ezster was dead had not come directly from Ezster herself but via a third person. She wondered whether it was possible that, for whatever reason, certain messages, if indeed they existed, might be passed from the spirit world through an intermediary.

Dying wish
A case of a reproachful ghost was recorded by Peter Moss in *Ghosts Over Britain* (1977). It concerned a mining family, the Brocks, who lived in Wintersville, Ohio. Gay, one of the five children, was very close to her mother, and when, in 1969, the latter died after a long illness, Gay, a vivacious girl of 17, was devastated. Before her mother had been admitted to hospital for the last time, she had asked Gay, who was the only child not working, to look after the family. But Gay, despite knowing she should honor her mother's dying wish, found herself unable to do so. Sunk in lethargy and depression, she lay in bed

Dr. Anna Peter
The Hungarian barrister was surprised that she was selected to receive the bedside visit from her mother's phantom — when she had never been particularly close to her in life.

▶ PAGE 85

THE CHAFFIN WILL

The aim of most ghosts with a message is to impart information about a death or a life-threatening crisis — but some are concerned with more mundane matters.

A DOUBLE WILL, an unexpected death, three disinherited brothers, an old Bible, a prophetic dream....These might be the key ingredients of a mystery novel, but they are in fact the key elements of one of the classic ghost-sighting cases published in 1928 in the *Proceedings* of the British Society for Psychical Research.

Division of property

On November 16, 1905, James L. Chaffin, a farmer of Davie County, North Carolina, and father of four sons, made a will, properly witnessed, leaving his entire estate, for reasons unknown, to his third son, Marshall. More than 13 years later, after reading in his Bible how Jacob cheated his elder brother Esau out of his heritage, Chaffin made a new will: "After reading the 27th chapter of Genesis, I, James L. Chaffin, do make my last will and testament... my little property [is] to be equally divided between my four children....And if she is living, you all must take care of your mammy....January 16, 1919."

Family Bible

The second will was unwitnessed, but in North Carolina it would be legally valid if it could be established that the whole document was in the testator's handwriting. Chaffin inserted the will in the old family Bible, at the relevant point in Genesis, folding over two pages to make a kind of pocket. Apparently, he never mentioned this new handwritten will to anyone.

On September 7, 1921, James L. Chaffin died. The only known will was that leaving everything to Marshall, and, since there were no apparent grounds for challenging it, Marshall had no difficulty in obtaining probate. He inherited his father's land and other property, and, following his death, a year after his father's, they passed to his widow and young son.

Father's message

In June 1925, the second son, James P. Chaffin, claimed that he began to have vivid dreams in which his father appeared and stood silently beside his bed. James, Jr., alleged that eventually the apparition, dressed in the black coat his son knew well, spoke: "You will find my

will in my overcoat pocket," it said. Then, claimed James, Jr., the apparition disappeared.

James and the eldest son John, to whom the coat had been given, found in a sewn-up inside pocket of the coat a message in their father's handwriting: "Read the 27th chapter of Genesis in my daddie's old Bible." The brothers, accompanied by witnesses, found the Bible in a drawer in their mother's house. As it was being taken out, it fell to the floor and, because of the folded pages, opened automatically where the will had been inserted. The handwriting was adjudged to be that of James L. Chaffin and the second, equal-share will was tendered for probate in 1925 at the local Davie County court.

Mocksville courthouse, Davie County, North Carolina
It was here that the controversial Chaffin will was tendered for probate. Ten witnesses were prepared to give evidence that the will was in the testator's handwriting, so the property was divided equally between James L. Chaffin's remaining children.

One of the interesting points about this case is that James, Jr., claimed that his father delivered his message to him in a dream. Some people might claim that dreams, occurring during sleep, do not strictly speaking belong to the world of apparitions. Yet James, Jr., appears to have seen the critical apparition of his father, the one that delivered the message, when he was, in his own words, "in a doze." And many ghost researchers believe that the twilight time between wakefulness and sleep is one in which many ghost sightings reportedly take place.

much of the day. She failed to prepare proper meals and neglected the house.

Late one morning, about a month after the funeral, as Gay lay half-asleep in bed, she became aware, she claimed, of a hand that was reaching around her bedroom door. The next moment, she said, the mattress sank, the springs creaked, and she felt someone heavy sitting on the bed. Then, Gay saw her mother sitting there, wearing her favorite red-and-black party dress. Her mother looked as real as she did in life, an

---

> **She saw her mother sitting there, wearing her favorite red-and-black party dress. Her mother looked as real as in life, an impression confirmed when Gay threw her arms around her and, she claimed, felt warm, solid flesh.**

---

impression confirmed when Gay threw her arms around her and, she claimed, felt warm, solid flesh and breathed in a familiar mingled scent of face powder, hair, perspiration, and cigarette smoke. According to Gay, her mother then extricated herself from her daughter's embrace and moved away from her down the bed. "Gay Agnes," she allegedly said, addressing her daughter by a name she used only at times of deep emotion, "shouldn't you be out there looking after them...you *did* promise...." Then, claimed Gay, the weight on the bed lifted, the springs creaked again, and her mother was no longer there.

Energy restored

Suddenly, Gay reported, she felt all her old life and energy restored to her: the apparition had shown her, she said, that although her mother had been invisible until then, her presence had always been in the house. Rousing herself, Gay set about performing the household tasks she had left neglected for so long.

A little later that morning, Gay claimed, another strange incident occurred. Gathering up the neglected laundry in the house, Gay threw it in the washing machine in the basement and went on to other jobs. An hour later she returned to the basement to wait for the washing cycle to finish. Astonished and fearful, she saw lying across a chair the dress that so recently she had seen her mother's ghost wearing. Certain that it had not been in the basement on her previous visit, she ran to telephone her father, who was at work. He insisted that she was mistaken — he had personally put the dress in a trunk in the loft. But, when Gay returned to the basement, the dress was still there. She picked it up. It was impregnated with her mother's characteristic odor. (A particularly curious feature of the Gay Brock case is the reportedly physical nature, uncommon in ghost sightings, of the apparition and its clothing.)

Guilty conscience?

What are we to make of Gay's account? Had the dress truly been removed and worn by a ghost? Or was there a rational explanation for the incident: had Gay's father been mistaken about the whereabouts of the dress, had it been in the basement all the time, and had Gay simply missed seeing it the first time? As to what she saw at her bedside, was this the spirit of her mother returning to chide her? Or was the phantom, as that in Janos Felker's case may have been, simply a subjective image projected by the subconscious in someone with a guilty conscience?

Mystery grave
Newly arrived in England, Gay Brock dreamt of visiting a grave. The grave- stone was of an unfamiliar English type. When she saw the same gravestone in a country churchyard, she interpreted the dream as a message from the deceased.

ALL IN A DREAM

It appears that some people have a greater capacity for psychic experience than others. Gay Brock seems to be such an "encounter-prone" personality, because after she married and moved to rural England, she reported another unusual incident. It started with a persistent dream that recurred several times a week over a period of about a month. In it Gay had images of herself kneeling beside an unfamiliar grave.

Grave inscription

One day, she was walking through St. Peter's churchyard in Coggeshall, Essex. Suddenly she stopped dead — for before her was the very grave she had seen so often in her dreams. Clearly neglected, the inscription on the headstone was almost illegible, but after clearing away the foliage, she read that a certain Nell Osborn, wife of Henry Coggeshall of New York, was buried there.

Who she was, Gay had no idea, but if the dream had disturbed her before, it now became an obsession. But one day, so she says, she knew what she had to do: She scraped the headstone, weeded and tidied up the gravel, and bought a heather plant. From that moment on, the dream ceased, and Gay felt that Nell Osborn was at peace at last.

CHAPTER FOUR

VISIONS OF THE LIVING

Phantoms appearing at the time of a person's death, perhaps to communicate with loved ones, are known as crisis apparitions. Yet there is an additional twist to this phenomenon: some apparitions appear to be of people who are alive.

Early one morning in 1977, Shirley Gray was awakened in her home in East Anglia, England, by a voice calling her name. She opened her eyes and saw, hovering above the foot of the bed, the head and shoulders of her friend Pat Craven. Craven appeared to be in pain or some form of distress, and to Gray it seemed that she had been through a grueling experience. But what Gray really noticed was what she was wearing. Usually a stylish dresser, Craven had on something that she would not normally be seen in

— a scruffy, square-cut garment with a ragged neckline. When she arose, Gray tried to contact her friend, but found out she was away vacationing in Kenya. She telephoned her home every day, and a week later finally spoke to Craven within hours of her return. The first question Gray asked was: "Whatever happened to you?"

Hospital gown

This was Craven's story: As a result of an accident in her hotel in Mombasa, she had been rushed to a hospital for an emergency operation on her Achilles tendon. For the operation she had been given a rough hospital gown — a crude square-cut garment with a ragged neckline — exactly like the sketch that Gray had drawn immediately after she had been awakened by the voice that same night.

This type of event, involving what appears to be some form of unexplained communication, might be termed a crisis apparition. For Pat Craven faced a crisis

> **Pat Craven faced a crisis in Kenya, and several thousand miles away, at reportedly the same time, Gray saw what seemed to be an apparition of Craven.**

In addition, the story has some interesting features. Craven and Gray were on Christmas-card terms, but were not particularly close. Thus Gray had not been lying in bed wondering how Craven was getting on in Kenya; in fact she did not even know that Craven was away. In much the same way, Craven, if she had consciously wanted to call for help (which she says she did not), would certainly have thought of other people before Gray. And yet Gray claims she was awakened by a call, and that she recognized Craven immediately. In addition, she drew a picture showing a remarkable likeness to the hospital gown that Craven was wearing, but that Gray, it seems, could not possibly have known about.

Imagination or reality?

How might this story be explained? Shirley Gray could simply have made it up. Yet if she concocted it after the event, how could she have persuaded her family and friends to support her claim that she knew that something was wrong before news arrived?

If she made up the story at the time, how could she know that Craven was in trouble just then? And how did she correctly guess what clothes she was wearing? The detailed information about the garment suggests that Gray's vision was more than coincidental.

Psychic messages

Is it possible for someone who is intensely worried to put out psychic "feelers" about the well-being of a loved one? Perhaps, but how would they know when to do so? This was not the case with Shirley Gray, for she was not very friendly with Pat Craven, and says she was definitely not worrying about her when she saw the apparition. It seems likely, in theory at least, that such apparitions are produced by people who are facing a crisis and that somehow the rush of adrenaline that occurs in such a

Shirley Gray (left) and Pat Craven

in Kenya, and several thousand miles away, at reportedly the same time, Gray saw what seemed to be an apparition of Craven, apparently reflecting the crisis. Yet unlike the crisis apparitions discussed in the previous chapter, this apparition did not herald a death.

situation might cause mental messages or pictures to be scattered far and wide.

As discussed in the previous chapter, reports of crisis apparitions increase dramatically during wartime and most take place at the time of death. However, a number do not signal a fatality. A good example of a living apparition was experienced by Mr. and Mrs. Almond in December 1943. Tom Almond was away fighting in North Africa. His wife, Violet, was at home in Norwich, England. She awoke one night, feeling that she was not alone. She looked up and saw the head and shoulders of her husband, Tom, floating above her head. She shut her eyes tight, but knew he was still there, a foot away. She opened them again, turned over on her side, and the image moved around, keeping in line with her eyes. Suddenly, it disappeared.

Frightened by the vision, and worried for her husband's safety, Violet jumped

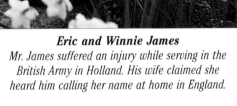

Eric and Winnie James
Mr. James suffered an injury while serving in the British Army in Holland. His wife claimed she heard him calling her name at home in England.

> # The times of the Almonds' experiences matched closely; just when Tom was in mortal danger in Africa, Violet apparently saw his ghostly form at home in Norwich.

out of bed and sat down to write Tom a letter. It crossed in the mail with one from him. He described how he had been caught under fire in no-man's-land.

As the shells came nearer, he knelt in prayer, asking God to return him safely to Violet. The times of the Almonds' experiences matched closely; just when Tom was in mortal danger in Africa, Violet apparently saw his ghostly form at home in Norwich.

The apparition reported by Mrs. Violet Almond might be called a classically simple hallucination. It involved just head and shoulders, and it stayed in front of her face when she turned her head. It sounds as if it might have been all in her imagination, and would not have been visible to anyone else present in the room. Yet apparitions seem to behave in all sorts of different ways. Some reportedly open doors; some look at people; some seem to avoid obstacles or walk through walls. Others are heard, but apparently not seen at all.

Painful injury
In Holland in 1944, for example, a gardener in civilian life, Eric James, was standing unsteadily in the hatch of a Sherman tank, holding on as it slithered on the icy road. When it went into a ditch, the steel cover clanged down on his left hand, almost severing the ring finger. "There was no pain for about ten minutes," he said. In the military hospital in Gent, the surgeon promised to do what he could to leave the hand useful for gardening. They operated in the early hours of the morning.

Back in Northamptonshire in England, James's wife, Winifred, knew nothing about her husband's injury, but was apparently awakened in the middle of the night when she heard his voice calling out her name. She sat up in bed with delight, thinking he had come home on leave, but she could see nothing.

BROTHERLY ADVICE
In her book *The Invisible Picture* (1981) the American psychic researcher Dr. Louisa Rhine reported an unusual case of a living apparition that reportedly took place during the First World War. A corporal in the Canadian Expeditionary Force had been captured in Germany. He tried to escape, was recaptured and beaten up, and escaped again. He walked 200 miles to the Dutch border, a hazardous journey over several days, during which he had little to eat. He reached a crossroads near the border in the middle of a snowstorm. He was in a state of exhaustion. He knew that if he went the right way he would soon be safely in Holland, but if he took the wrong road he might run into a German patrol.

Sense of direction
He was desperately exhausted, and he had no idea which road to take. And so he set off one way at random. Suddenly, he said, his brother stepped out into his path and said, "No, Dick, not that way. Take the other road, you damned fool!" He took the advice, and was soon safe over the border. His brother was hundreds of miles away at the time and unaware of having been so helpful.

The most unusual aspect of this reported crisis apparition was that the vision came to the man undergoing the crisis, rather than the other way round.

THE WOMAN IN GRAY

Miss J. B. from the village of Blubberhouses, England, submitted the following story to the magazine *Man, Myth and Magic* in the late 1960's.

Just after the First World War Miss J. B. was living with her parents in a large old farmhouse in the Yorkshire Dales. "I must have been about six when I saw my 'ghost,'" Miss J. B. recalled. "She was thin and pale, with long dark hair tied in a bun at the nape of her neck, and she stood by the kitchen range sobbing and muttering in a language I could not understand. Her dress was gray and worn, but she had an air of gentility about her."

Grief-stricken

Miss J. B. said that she saw the figure again about a year later, and subsequently saw her, always weeping, about nine or ten times during the next 10 years.

When she was in her teens, Miss J. B. went to live with a relative in Ireland, and did not return to Yorkshire until 1945. As she and her mother were driving home, her mother explained that, as the place was too big for her following her father's death, she had taken in a family of Polish refugees as boarders — a mother and two young daughters. The father, she said, had vanished during the German occupation, and the mother was grief-stricken. When they entered the kitchen, there — to Miss J. B.'s astonishment — was the "lady in gray" of her youth, standing and weeping.

Benign intelligence

Miss J. B. reportedly believed that the vision she had had as a child was not transmitted by the Polish woman herself, whose grief, after all, was not caused until years after the apparition occurred, "but from some benign intelligence — Heaven or God, if you like — that, with the knowledge of what was to come, wanted to build up sympathy in me in advance."

The operation was successful, as the surgeon told Eric when he spoke to him later that morning. "By the way," he asked, "who's Winnie? You kept calling her name all through the operation."

Sympathy pains

In the case of the Bougheys the curious message went in the other direction. Husband Les was in Egypt with the Royal Air Force, living in a tent at El Firdan. One night he woke up with terrible pain in the first finger of his left hand. He could not remember injuring it; nor was there a wound or bite mark, but the pain was so bad that his tent-mate, Jock, went out to get a mug of cold water, and Les sat up half the night with his finger in the water, trying to ease the pain.

What he did not know was that in England at the factory in Cheshire where his wife, May, worked, she had caught a piece of metal in her finger. It had become infected, and she had had to go to the doctor to get it lanced. Les Boughey woke up in Egypt at exactly the same time May was sitting in the doctor's surgery, waiting for the doctor's knife to relieve the awful throbbing pain in the first finger of her left hand.

Message of hope

Although war generates many crises, not all are bad. In her book, *Understanding Ghosts* (1980), Canadian psychic researcher and writer Victoria Branden tells of the experience of a friend during the Second World War.

The woman's husband was away serving with the armed forces in England. She was ironing, and the children were, unusually, quietly busy with their homework. She felt as if she were in a kind of dreamlike state, the kind that one can easily slip into when doing menial work that requires little or no mental effort. She said that the door of the house suddenly opened, and there was her husband standing in uniform. Yet before she could speak, or react in

any way, he vanished. She put down the iron and tottered to a chair, almost fainting. The children crowded around, concerned, asking what had happened. They, of course, had been concentrating

Psychic researcher Victoria Branden

on their homework and, perhaps as a result, had seen nothing; for them, the door simply had not opened at all.

They all talked about it, and were very concerned that her husband and their father had been killed. They made a note of the time and the circumstances, but could do no more, since transatlantic telephone calls were impossible. Thus they waited for news, in an agony of apprehension.

The news turned out to be good. On the same day that the woman had said she had seen her husband, he had been told that he was to be sent to Canada on a training program. This meant he would be well away from battle and able to see his family. It was a moment of intense emotion. He did not consciously try to send his wife a message, but she seemed to get it anyway.

Word of warning

Occasionally, an apparition seems to bring a useful warning of impending crisis. Author Andrew MacKenzie cited

> She said that the door of the house suddenly opened, and there was her husband standing in uniform. Yet before she could speak, or react in any way, he vanished.

▸ PAGE 92

GHOSTLY CENSUS

When the British Society for Psychical Research carried out its "Census of Hallucinations" in the 19th century, it was revealed that the majority of the "ghosts" reported were of people who were still alive.

FOUNDED IN LONDON in 1882 by a group of distinguished academics, the British Society for Psychical Research set itself a primary goal of investigating apparitions. Members wrote letters to friends, colleagues, and journals, asking for ghost-related information. They were deluged with material, and after doing their best to reject stories that lacked supporting evidence, they were left with an impressive number of what might be called "authenticated" cases.

Major survey

In 1886, a 1,400-page survey was published by the British Society for Psychical Research. Called *Phantasms of the Living*, it was compiled by Cambridge classicist Edmund Gurney, poet, critic and essayist Frederic Myers (also from Cambridge), and researcher Frank Podmore. They said that they were trying with this collection of 702 cases to indicate that apparitions might be real, and to lay the foundation for a thorough study of such ghostly encounters.

Myers, who had invented the word "telepathy" in order to describe the transfer of thoughts, without vocalization, from one person's mind to another, suggested that the witness of the apparition might simply be receiving a telepathic signal from the person represented by the apparition, who was not present in any real sense. "Instead of describing a ghost as a dead person permitted to communicate with the living," he explained, "let us define it as a manifestation of persistent personal energy." In a further definition of psychical terms, Myers and his colleagues called the person who claimed to see the apparition "the percipient," and the person reportedly sending out an image of the apparition "the agent."

More than half of the 702 cases reported in the book had occurred near to a moment of death or other serious crisis. The frequency of the sighting of apparitions at a time of crisis seemed to suggest that such circumstances might, in theory at least, provoke or permit telepathic communication.

Henry Sidgwick

Henry Sidgwick, professor of moral philosophy at Cambridge University, was the first president of the British Society for Psychical Research. He spent five years trying to find out what proportion of the general population had seen ghosts, and what sort of ghosts they had seen. He had census forms printed that displayed in effect a single question: "Have you seen a ghost? If so, please write your name and address below." When he received the name and address, he sent out more forms for further details of the alleged sightings.

Sidgwick found more than 400 people to distribute the census forms, and received an amazing 17,000 replies, from Italy, Austria, France, Germany, and Brazil, as well as from Britain. Among these replies, 1,684 — almost 10 percent — claimed to have encountered a ghost! About 1,000 said they had seen one, 500 that they had heard one, and 2 claimed to have been touched. Surprisingly enough, 129 of the phantoms had reportedly been perceived by more than one person.

This disproved many commonly held notions about ghosts. Not only did one person in ten claim to have seen one, but the majority were the ghosts of people who were still alive, even if many were near death.

> **Sidgwick had forms printed that displayed in effect a single question: "Have you seen a ghost? If so, please write your name and address below."**

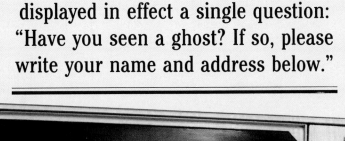

Society for Psychical Research

NIGHT WALKERS

Researchers Celia Green and Charles McCreery recorded the following case in their book *Apparitions* (1975): A woman reported that when her husband was out late with the boys, she went to bed at midnight.

Alcoholic influence

He came back at 2 A.M., so much the worse for wear that she had to let him in, and help him upstairs to bed. Within a few minutes she became aware of movement on his side of the bed, and, in the bright moonlight, saw him in his pajamas rising swiftly to nearly full height, but slightly bent at the waist, as if ready to run. She put a hand out to stop him — then realized that she was leaning on him; he was still in bed, fast asleep.

Arthur C. Clarke
In addition to his scientific studies, Clarke wrote a number of highly successful science fiction novels.

just such a case in his book *Apparitions and Ghosts* (1971): In 1951 Helen Crone was working in her kitchen in West London when she saw the head and shoulders of a friend, who looked extremely anxious, and somehow managed to suggest that she should go into her dining room.

There Mrs. Crone found that her baby son, John, had rocked his pram forward to a buffet, had reached into a drawer, and was now playing with several razor-sharp knives.

Clarke's theory

Scientist Arthur C. Clarke suggested a possible explanation for apparitions of the living in his television series, *Arthur C. Clarke's World of Strange Powers*. He pointed out that the eye is like a camera, for it uses a lens to focus images of the outside world on a sensitive screen called the retina, and there information is transmitted to the brain along the optic nerve. From this information, processed in the brain, we form our picture of the world outside. Suppose the system could sometimes work in reverse, Clarke suggested, so that the brain sent images to the eye, transforming the retina into a kind of television screen. Then believing would, in a sense, become seeing. This reverse operation, Clarke maintains, might be

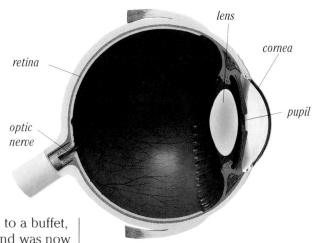

The miracle of sight
This diagram illustrates the various parts of the eye that help the brain produce an eventual image. Arthur C. Clarke suggested that a reverse process might take place — an image may be formulated first in the brain, and then transmitted to the eye.

triggered by any number of things — grief, worry, drugs, exhaustion, stress, or merely by an overactive imagination.

Multiple witnesses

So are apparitions of those who are alive real, or just a figment of the viewer's imagination? There is no real proof of Clarke's hypothesis, but if it were corrrect, then the apparitions people see

> If Clarke's hypothesis were corrrect, then the apparitions people see might be real images, but images formed only on their own retinas, and therefore invisible to anyone else.

might be real images, but images formed only on their own retinas, and therefore invisible to anyone else. Yet this poses an interesting question: How can one explain the 129 ghosts seen by more than one person reported to the Society for Psychical Research in the 19th century in their "Census of Hallucinations"?

LOOKING FOR CLUES

Numerous theories have been formulated to explain the ghost-seeing experience. It seems likely that, in some cases, our perception of reality becomes confused through the complex workings of the eye and the brain.

THE EXPERIENCE OF SIGHT relies very much on the mind's perception of what the eye has seen. A central problem with visual perception is how the brain interprets visual patterns. When two people look at the same object, they may well see two different images, depending on how the brain interprets the information it is presented with. But each person probably believes that what he or she has seen is a truthful representation of the scene. In many cases, it is easy to understand how the brain can be misled as to what the eye is viewing. An enigmatic geometric pattern, a confusion of perspective, or a trick of the light, can all radically mislead the viewer.

A sense of perspective
Numerous visual experiments prove how easily the eye may be deceived. Even in the 18th century, English artist William Hogarth

Strange outlook
William Hogarth's engraving of a fisherman (1754) mixes perspectives and views to create an impossible scene.

(1697–1764) engraved and painted pictures with the specific intention of combining various views and perspectives to produce theoretically impossible scenes. At first glance the viewer may take Hogarth's pictures at face value; it is only on closer examination that he or she notices the irregularities. Hogarth's deceptive pictures illustrate how easily the principles of perspective can be manipulated.

A 20th-century example of visual misinformation was created by American psychologist E. G. Boring. The image he conceived can be seen as two quite different people: a coy young woman from one angle, or a rather frightening old hag from another. Even when the viewer fixes the image with a steady gaze, it still changes. The differing perceptions originate in the brain and are not due to a change in the information being supplied to the eye.

Deceiving the brain
When considering possible witnesses' reports of apparitions, it is important to realize how easily the brain can misinterpret information being supplied by the eye, particularly when such sightings take place in poor light and when the viewer is either tired or under stress, and may have a strong desire to make contact with the subject. Richard Gregory, director of the brain and perception laboratory at Bristol University, in England, made this observation in his book *The Intelligent Eye* (1970): "Sensory information is so incomplete....Given the slenderest clues to the nature of surrounding objects, we identify them and act not so much according to what is directly sensed, *but to what is believed.*"

The odd couple
E. G. Boring's confusing image of two very different women.

OUT OF TIME

You hear a car pull up outside your home and you rush to the door to greet these unexpected visitors — but there's nobody there. A short time later, your guests do arrive and are amazed when you say you were expecting them. Might such cases of false arrival be due to time slips, psychic energy, or simply a vivid imagination?

ONE SPRING DAY IN 1915, Alice Bartlett, a chambermaid at the Great Central hotel in London, was sweeping room 338. She said that she saw the hotel parcels boy appear in the doorway, five feet from her, so naturally she asked, "Parcel for me, Charlie?" According to the author and ghost-hunter, Andrew MacKenzie, who recounted what happened next in his book, *Apparitions and Ghosts* (1971), the boy did not reply. Bartlett claimed that as she started toward him, his figure recoiled, then disappeared.

Prior departure

When the case was investigated further, it was found that the parcels boy had left the hotel two weeks earlier. A similar, but more detailed, case that occurred on January 1886, is recorded in *Phantasms of the Living*, the British Society for Psychical Research's publication,

The entrance hall of the Great Central hotel, London

compiled by Edmund Gurney, Frederic Myers, and Frank Podmore. Mrs. Augusta Gladstone of Shedfield Cottage, Botley, England, went to visit an old, sick neighbor, who lived half a mile away. "Mrs. Bedford was ill in bed, and I went upstairs to see her," Mrs. Gladstone told the Society for Psychical Research's investigator. "Whilst I was there, the thought struck me that the light from the window, which was opposite the foot of the bed, was too strong for the invalid; and I determined, without saying a word about it to either

Choral story
It was in this church in Windsor that a chorister, Mrs. Allan, says she heard phantom footsteps.

HEAVY FOOTSTEPS
Some false arrival cases seem to be triggered by a crisis – sometimes even a minor one. A good example is described in Andrew MacKenzie's book, *Apparitions and Ghosts* (1971). In the early 1950's, 21-year-old choir member Mrs. Allan was waiting for choir practice to begin at the church of St. Andrew and St. Peter, in Windsor, England, when she says she heard hurried heavy footsteps. She looked around and saw a fellow choir member, Miss Simpson, rushing past the altar rails and thought: "What a racket, and not very respectful. After all, she's in plenty of time."

More haste, less speed
A few minutes later the choirmaster called them to order and asked where Miss Simpson was. Mrs. Allan said she had arrived, but no one could find any sign of her in the church. Ten minutes later Miss Simpson ran into the church with a bandaged hand. She had cut it while hurriedly preparing a meal and so had been delayed.

Mr. or Mrs. Bedford, to give her a curtain."

The next morning Mrs. Gladstone took a piece of serge from a cupboard in her dressing room and held it up with both hands to check the length, but said to herself: "It's not long enough." On Monday afternoon she returned to visit the old couple, but saw only Mr. Bedford downstairs. After a few remarks, he said his wife had seen her on Sunday morning; Mrs. Bedford had told her husband that she had "seen" Mrs. Gladstone holding up a curtain with both hands. Next, claimed Mrs. Bedford, Mrs. Gladstone had said it was not long enough, had smiled – and disappeared.

Time travel
Both these cases appear to illustrate the sighting of an apparition that involves some form of what might be called a time slip. It is certainly possible that the parcels boy at the Great Central hotel had entered room 338 at some point in the past with a package for the occupant, and it is clear that Mrs. Gladstone had held up the piece of material and noted that it was not the right size. Yet other people, in different locations, had apparently visualized these very actions. Is it possible that they had actually "seen" these people, or were they somehow picking up on a bizarre form of mental impression, message, or picture?

In 1954 the scholarly author Canon J. B. Phillips reported an intriguing event that occurred at a conference center in the mountains above Los Angeles. Like the parcels boy tale, this story was later recorded in Andrew MacKenzie's book *Apparitions and Ghosts*. The canon was staying in a remote chalet with his wife, young daughter, and secretary. During the course of one evening his secretary ran to fetch something, tripped, fell, and

hit her head. Not knowing whether the injury was serious, the canon radioed for an ambulance, and Mrs. Phillips was taken with the young lady in the ambulance to the hospital.

The canon, worried, prayed for his secretary's health, then lay down to rest. At 11 P.M. he said he heard the sound of a car driving up the dusty road outside the chalet and his wife saying: "Thank you very much...goodnight," and the slam of a car door. He ran out to welcome his wife back and ask for news – but there was no one there. The road, so he said, was quite deserted.

The same sounds
The canon was perplexed, yet somehow felt that all would be well. He went back to bed, and slept for an hour. At midnight, or a minute or two afterwards, he heard precisely the same sounds, rushed out of the chalet, and found that his wife had been brought back by a friend. His secretary had not been

> ## "I followed him into the passage and turned into the ante-room...where I expected to find him. On opening the door, to my great surprise, he was not there."

seriously injured, though she had been detained at the hospital for 24 hours.

This puzzling event is a good example of what the British Society for Psychical Research classified as a false arrival.

Military mis-arrival
There are occasions, however, when the pattern is slightly different – apparitions may be clearly seen, even when the arrival is unexpected.

On February 20, 1847, Maj. William Bigge, of the British Army's 70th (Surrey) Regiment, reported that at about 3 P.M., he was walking from his quarters in Templemore, Ireland, to mail some letters, when he saw Colonel Reed, about 50 feet away, walking toward the messhall door, through which he then entered. He was dressed in a brown shooting jacket and regulation tweed trousers, and was carrying a fishing rod and a landing net. In a report Bigge wrote for Edmund Gurney, who published it in *Phantasms of the Living*, he wrote: "...anxious to speak to him...I followed him into the passage and turned into the ante-room on the left-hand side, where I expected to find him. On opening the door, to my great surprise, he was not there; the only person in the room was Quartermaster

---

He said that he had never had "the slightest hallucination of the senses on any other occasion."

Nolan, 70th Regiment, and I immediately asked him if he had seen the colonel, and he replied he had not."

Bigge was astonished by this apparent disappearance, and discussed it at once in the barrackyard with Lieutenant Caulfield of the 66th Regiment. They were still talking about it 10 minutes later, when the colonel appeared, walking into the barracks from the opposite direction. He was wearing precisely the same clothes Bigge had described to Caulfield and was accompanied by another officer. He said he had been fishing for at least two hours and had not been near the messhall all afternoon.

Major misunderstanding
Major Bigge was deeply concerned by this apparent misunderstanding. He said that he had never had "the slightest hallucination of the senses on any other occasion," but was convinced that the figure he saw was indeed that of Colonel Reed. "I was not aware that he had gone out fishing — a very unusual thing to do at this time of the year; neither had I seen him before in the dress I have described during that day," he declared. "My eyesight being very good, and the colonel's figure and general appearance somewhat

remarkable, it is morally impossible that I could have mistaken any other person in the world for him. That I *did* see him I shall continue to believe until the last day of my existence."

Thread of energy
In attempting to explain the major's experience, Edmund Gurney suggests that since Colonel Reed was actually approaching the barracks, with his thoughts more or less consciously turned in that direction, Bigge might have picked up on what Gurney called some slender thread of approaching energy. "If there is any justification at all for the provisional hypothesis that the sense of impending arrival is a condition favourable for the emission of a telepathical influence," he wrote, "it is of importance that, at the time when the phantasmal form was seen, Colonel Reed was not busy with his fishing, but was rapidly approaching his destination." Those of a skeptical nature, on the other hand, might easily argue Bigge's case as being one of pure hallucination, but the timing, and such curious details as the description of the colonel's clothes, might disprove such an explanation.

NORWEGIAN TRICKSTER
There is a remarkable parallel between cases of false arrivals and apparitions of what are known as doubles, or ghostly images of oneself. One such is the *vardogr*, or spectral double, of Norwegian folklore. The arrival of a father's vardogr was described in 1917 by Weirs Jensen, editor of the *Journal* of the Norwegian Society for Psychical Research: "The possessor of a Vardogr announces his arrival. His steps are heard on the staircase. He is heard to unlock the door, kick off his overshoes, put his walking stick in place...." Then, apparently, the family open the door to welcome their father — and find no one there. The vardogr has, as usual, played a trick on them. Ten minutes later the man arrives.

Personal vardogr
Brad Steiger, American psychic investigator and author of Scandinavian descent, found in 1967 that he seemed to have a vardogr of his own. After an absence of two weeks, he arrived home at 2:30 A.M., tired from his long journey. He was surprised to find the lights on and his wife awake and waiting. She claimed she had been awakened by the sound of the front door opening, suitcases being set down, and the shuffling of footsteps.

She had come downstairs to greet her husband, only to find the hallway dark and empty. She then sat down on the sofa in the living room and tried to puzzle out what the strange sounds could have been. Shortly afterward, the car arrived, and the sounds were repeated, but this time with Steiger in attendance.

Regimental attire
In the 19th century, British soldiers of the 70th Regiment normally wore this type of uniform. What is convincing about Major Bigge's story of seeing his colonel in apparitional form, is that he described Colonel Reed's ghost as being dressed in very different clothes: the fishing outfit he in fact appeared in 10 minutes later.

PERSONAL VIEWS

The Norwegian vardogr and the German doppelgänger are both a type of "double" — that is, an alleged apparition of oneself. Opinions are divided as to the nature of such a bizarre phenomenon — some suggest that it may be related to such strange things as astral travel and out-of-body experiences (OBE's).

ON OCTOBER 3, 1863, Mr. S. R. Wilmot sailed from Liverpool for New York on the steamer *City of Limerick*. Mr. Wilmot's wife and children were then in Watertown, Connecticut. In the early hours of Wednesday, October 14, Wilmot had a vivid dream, in which his wife came to the door of the stateroom, wearing her nightgown. At the door she hesitated a little, when she noticed that her husband was not the only occupant of the room. Then she walked over to his bunk, bent down, kissed him, and after caressing him for a few moments, quietly withdrew.

Wilmot shared a cabin with another man, whose bunk was higher but farther from the door. In the morning, Wilmot's cabinmate commented on how lucky he was to be visited by a lovely woman in the night. Clearly the reported apparition was real enough to be visible to a bystander as well as to Mr. Wilmot.

Across the water

After reaching New York, Wilmot traveled on to Watertown. As soon as they were alone, his wife asked, strangely enough, whether he had received a visit from her the week before. She went on to say that she had been worrying about him, because another ship had run aground. So on that Tuesday night she lay awake, thinking about him, and at about four in the morning, she said, she seemed to go out looking for him. Somehow she crossed the stormy sea and reached a

The steamer City of Limerick

> On that Tuesday night she lay awake, thinking about him, and at about four in the morning... she seemed to go out looking for him. Somehow she crossed the stormy sea and reached a steamship.

A YOUNGER LOOK

Mrs. Caroline D. Larsen claimed to have had many out-of-body experiences. The following account appeared in her book *My Travels in the Spirit World*, which was published in 1927.

It was a gloomy night in the fall of 1918 and Caroline Larsen decided to retire early. She was unaware of falling asleep, and the next thing she knew she was standing in her room looking at her body lying in bed. She noted that she looked deathly pale, although everything else about the bedroom appeared to be normal.

Youthful reflection

She started to move around, and headed in the direction of the bathroom. As she crossed the landing she could hear her musician husband, Prof. Alfred Larsen, rehearsing downstairs. She claimed that she recognized the piece of music he and his fellow musicians were playing: the *Adagio* from Beethoven's Opus 127 Quartet. Once in the bathroom Mrs. Larsen saw her reflection in the mirror above the sink. What she saw left her aghast. She did not see the middle-aged woman she was expecting, but rather was confronted by her 18-year-old self.

Reluctant return

She decided to go downstairs and present her youthful self to her husband and his musical colleagues. But her progress was halted by a woman in shiny clothes who barred her passage. According to Mrs. Larsen, the woman pointed dramatically in the direction of her bedroom and said, "Where are you going? Go back to your body!" Mrs. Larsen reported that she sensed she should not argue with this command, and reluctantly she returned to her room, where she found her still-lifeless body. With a certain feeling of regret, she claims she reentered her body.

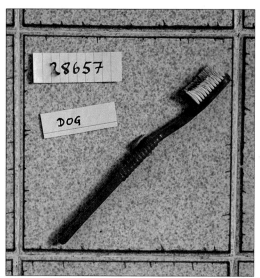

Off the wall
Dr. Blackmore attached a different number, word, and object to her kitchen wall each week in an attempt to prove the existence of out-of-body experiences (OBE's). A friend who claimed to experience OBE's was supposed to send her a postcard with the correct information.

ASTRAL TEST

British parapsychologist Dr. Susan Blackmore devised a simple experiment to test for the reality of out-of-body experiences, or OBE's. She was living in a cottage near Bristol, and a friend lived on the south coast of England, 100 miles away. The friend claimed he could have OBE's at will. Easy to claim, but could he prove it?

Still waiting

In a corner of Dr. Blackmore's kitchen, out of sight of the window, she stuck three things on the wall – a card with a five-digit number written on it, a card that contained a short word, and a small object. All the friend had to do was to send her a postcard saying "28657/DOG/toothbrush," and she could be sure that he had actually seen the things. Every week she changed the number, the word, and the object, so that the chance of his guessing what might be there next time was very small.

Nearly 10 years after the experiment began, Dr. Blackmore was still waiting for the postcard.

steamship. Mrs. Wilmot claimed she had never seen the ship before, but seemed to describe it with uncanny detail. She eventually found her husband's stateroom, but was startled to find another man sharing it. She described the man's bunk as set higher but further from the door. For a moment she was afraid, but she plucked up her courage, went over to her husband's side, bent down and embraced him, and then left the cabin to make her return journey home.

Perhaps the Wilmots made the story up, long after the event – but if not, what a story! Did Mrs. Wilmot really travel not only in her mind but with an apparition as well, across a thousand miles of Atlantic Ocean? It is also worth noting that the apparition not only found the right stateroom, but was reportedly seen by the man in the other bunk.

Reciprocal cases

In 1956 the Wilmots' story was featured in the British Society for Psychical Research's *Proceedings*. The Society's literature has reported several such "reciprocal cases," which seem to be observed by the parties at both ends of the alleged psychic link. James Cotter Morison reported an event that took place on June 18, 1883. He related that his mother and grandmother were engaged on a domestic matter in the dining room of their house on the Isle of Wight and had hoped that they would not be disturbed. Suddenly they were startled by a sharp knock on the front door. Morison's grandmother went to open it, planning to take the visitor into the drawing room. Not only was there no one at the door; there was no one in the long corridor

that led to the dining room. His mother remembered for years the look of astonishment on his grandmother's face.

A few days later they received a letter saying that the grandmother's sister had been near death in London, and would appreciate a visit. So Morison's grandmother went up to see her sister, and after exchanging greetings, she said: "Do you know, such a strange thing occurred, exactly at the time, it seems, when you were supposed to be dead, or dying."

"I know what you are going to say," said her sister. "When I was in the trance which was mistaken for my death, I thought I went to your house in the Isle of Wight and knocked at your dining room door. You opened it instantly, and looked much affrighted at not seeing me – or anyone – though I saw you!"

Auditory projection?

The sister, if this story is to be believed, seems to have projected an apparition real enough to startle her family by knocking on the door, yet not real enough to be visible. However, if she were merely hallucinating, it is possible to speculate that she would surely have imagined that her family would be able to see her. On the other side, mother and daughter said they heard the knock....

On December 23, 1935, Walter McBride was working on his farm near Indian Springs, Nevada. Throughout the day McBride found his thoughts turning to his father, who lived two miles away in the family home. He became increasingly concerned by these constant thoughts, and by the time he went to bed at 8 P.M. he was seriously worried about his father's well-being. Then, while he was still awake, he reportedly felt himself leaving his body.

His floating form, he claimed, was not restrained by walls, and he was soon traveling beyond the house and heading north toward his father's home. Before long he found himself gazing at his father, who was lying awake in bed, and staring

> **Not only was there no one at the door; there was no one in the long corridor....His mother remembered for years the look of astonishment on his grandmother's face.**

◆ PAGE·102

MIRROR IMAGE

Seeing an apparition is an extraordinary experience. But how much stranger when the phantom appears as a doppelgänger: an exact replica of yourself.

A YOUNG SWISS STUDENT, Boru, whose story was reported in Gabriel Delanne's *Fantômes de Vivants* (*Living Ghosts*) (1909), was working at his desk, when he needed to consult a reference book in the next room. He got up and went next door, found the book, and stood holding it in one hand, his other hand resting on the door knob between the two rooms.

Double vision

Suddenly he looked up and saw himself sitting at the desk, writing the same phrase that he had just looked up in the book. "The vision was in perfect detail; but what was most extraordinary was this: I was perfectly conscious of standing by the door, and the cold metal of the knob in my hand, while at the same time I had the sensation of sitting in a chair and using my pen to write with. I could read the phrase the seated-me was

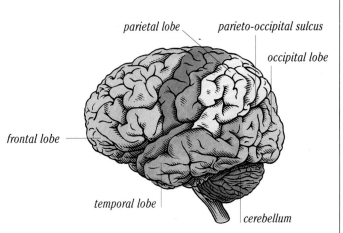

Brain function
Neurologists believe that the experience of seeing oneself originates from an irritation in the brain in the parieto-temporal-occipital area.

Leaving the body
Some people believe that astral travel may present a possible explanation for the doppelgänger phenomenon.

writing even though the other-me was 10 feet away. I returned to my desk and nothing was left of my double: I suppose Boru-1 and Boru-2 became one again."

So what are the various explanations for this bizarre phenomenon? It has been claimed that we all have an exact physical counterpart somewhere on earth. (Some folklore even maintains that coming face to face with your unknown twin results in certain death.) A phenomenon known as a time slip could be another explanation. Might it be possible for some people to be caught up in some strange hiccup in time and to witness themselves either in the past or the future?

Skeptics declare that seeing the image of oneself is a trick of the brain. Neurologists recognize autoscopy — the technical word for seeing oneself — as a symptom of migraine and epilepsy. Clearly some kind of explanation in terms of brain function is called for. It has been suggested, for example, that it involves an irritation in the parieto-temporal-occipital area of the brain.

Dinner partner

But we still have to learn why some people's migraine headaches produce this effect, while other people's do not. Harold C. of Chicago had experienced several instances of the doppelgänger effect, always associated with his migraine attacks. One day in 1958 he came home after work suffering from an attack of migraine. He sat down for dinner and saw, sitting opposite him, an exact replica of himself, who copied his every movement. The double stayed with him throughout the meal and then apparently vanished.

Believers in astral travel state that it is possible for the spiritual or astral body to leave the physical body and observe it from a distance; they put this idea forward as an explanation for the sighting of a doppelgänger. Whatever the truth may be, it is hard to imagine a more unsettling experience than leaving your body and coming face to face with yourself.

Lady Beresford
The owner of Ballachulish house was shocked to discover that the lady who was renting her home was also the woman who haunted her bedroom.

Lady Beresford suggested that the Boultons should use her bedroom while occupying the house, although she cautioned that it seemed to be haunted by the figure of a little woman.

incredulously in his son's direction. As soon as McBride realized that his father was in good health, he reportedly began his homeward journey. Once back in his own bedroom he said that he reentered his body, and instantly felt fully alert and wide awake. As a result he leapt out of bed and wrote down the details of his uncanny experience.

Two days later Walter traveled to his father's house to celebrate Christmas. His father told him that he had indeed seen Walter standing at the foot of his bed, and that he too had been prompted to write down the exact time and details of the apparition. Two other Christmas houseguests, Mrs. J. E. Wires and her son Earl from Shoals, Indiana, verified this story and signed a statement saying: "I can vouch the above-described meeting and discussion did take place."

Scottish phantom
OBE's or astral travel, if indeed they existed, could certainly help to explain some of the more puzzling accounts of apparitions, including the baffling tale of Mrs. Boulton, Lady Beresford, and the bedroom phantom of Ballachulish.

In the late 19th century this story was sent by a Mr. Boulton to the

Ballachulish House
Standing near the banks of Loch Linnhe in the Scottish Highlands, this imposing building has a history of hauntings — including sightings of a phantom on horseback who gallops to the main door, dismounts, and then vanishes.

English current affairs periodical called *The Spectator*. His wife, he said, had dreamt several times about a house. She did not know where the house was, but she visited it frequently in these dreams, and was able to walk through it and describe the contents of the rooms in considerable detail.

Summer residence
In the autumn of 1883 Mr. Boulton heard that Lady Beresford, a local dignitary and owner of Ballachulish House, was planning to spend some time in the south. He at once wrote to ask whether he and his wife might be allowed to rent her home for the summer. She seemed to be agreeably disposed toward the plan, and he went up to finalize the details. Lady Beresford suggested that the Boultons should use her bedroom while occupying the house, although she cautioned that it seemed to be haunted by the figure of a little woman.

When Mrs. Boulton arrived a few days afterwards, she was astonished to find that this was the house she had seen in her dreams. In room after room, everything was just as she remembered. She even stopped outside a door and gave her husband a detailed description of the contents, before she went into that room.

However, the most remarkable aspect of the whole story was the meeting a few days later between Mrs. Boulton and the owner of the house; the moment Lady Beresford set eyes on Mrs. Boulton, she said "My goodness! You are the woman who haunts my bedroom!"

THE LONG MARCH

"Somehow I kept turning and marching but I was no longer there. Eventually the torture ended...."

IN THE EARLY 1980's Mr. W. Lee, from Bridgnorth, England, submitted to the British magazine of the paranormal *The Unexplained* the following account of his experience of astral travel.

"It was 1963. I was in the [British] army and not very happy about it. I rebelled and had to be punished from time to time. Pack drill (being marched across a drill square at a very fast pace with a pack full of house bricks) had been abolished but a particularly sadistic sergeant decided to put four of us on pack drill. It was a very hot day and he stood at the edge of the square while a lance corporal marched us, at incredible speed, up and down the square.

"One of the lads suffered from asthma and kept collapsing, while myself and two others were kept at it. I was determined not to let either the sergeant or the two older soldiers see that I was suffering so I just kept going while the commands being shouted at us grew dimmer and dimmer. In the end I could not hear them. My heart did not seem to be beating and I could not see. Somehow I kept turning and marching but I was no longer there. Eventually the torture ended and I thought that was all there was to it — until I returned home.

Astral double?

"My mother then told me a fascinating story. On the day that I had been undergoing this on the drill square my mother and younger brother had been doing some shopping. They were about 100 yards from the nearest bus stop to our home when a bus stopped and I got off in my army uniform! She called to me as I walked up the road but I did not answer or turn round....Confused as to why I did not respond to their calls [they] ran to try and catch me up, because I was walking very quickly. I rounded the corner four or five seconds ahead of them and when they too came round the corner I had disappeared. There was only a postman to be seen. My mother asked where the soldier had gone and he told her nobody had come round the corner.

"The only reason I can think of for its happening is that at the time I was under severe stress. I know...that to appear in the 'astral' is by no means unusual — and my mother and brother did see me get off that bus."

CHAPTER FIVE

THE PHANTOM TRAIL

Centuries of investigation into the ghost phenomenon has shown how easy it is to be swayed by the vivid accounts of imaginative witnesses. A methodical, down-to-earth approach is more valuable to an investigator than any ghostbusting paraphernalia.

In 1883 the British diplomat, Frederick Temple Hamilton-Temple-Blackwood, first marquis of Dufferin and Ava, was staying in a large house in County Offaly in Ireland. Lord Dufferin was awakened one night by blood-curdling sounds in the gardens. He decided to investigate and, not without considerable trepidation, looked out the window to the moonlit gardens beyond. The terrifying sounds he had heard were coming from the shadows cast by a group of trees, and as he strained to see what

> It became apparent that the tale was simply part of Lord Dufferin's after-dinner repertoire, and that one impressionable listener took him too seriously.

horrors they concealed, a man emerged struggling under the weight of a coffin. Dufferin leaped out of the window and raced across the lawn toward the figure. As he approached, the intruder raised his head, revealing a ghastly expression. Dufferin tried to confront the man, only to pass right through him — and when he turned around both the man and his gruesome load had vanished.

Over the years the horror of this ghost sighting passed, but Dufferin knew he would never be able to forget the tortured face of his ghostly visitor.

Fatal ascent

Ten years later, Dufferin, who was then British ambassador to France, was attending an official function at the Grand Hotel in Paris. As he went to take the elevator to the reception on the top floor, he recoiled in horror — the elevator operator was the double of the ghoulish figure he had seen a decade earlier. Dufferin stood back and let the elevator doors close. But the passengers who were inside never made it to the top floor — the supporting cable snapped and all the occupants were killed.

This is, without doubt, a wonderful ghost story — a British lord escapes certain death

Lord Dufferin

as a result of a chilling ghostly encounter that took place years before. But despite the fact that the account was endorsed by several psychic investigators and has appeared in many apparently reputable publications, there is not one shred of evidence to support the story. When Melvin Harris, the British author and investigator of the paranormal, conducted research into the case, it became apparent that the tale was simply part of Lord Dufferin's after-dinner repertoire, and that one impressionable listener took him too seriously. The same tale has also been found in 10 distinctly different versions, set in various parts of Britain, France, and the United States. Not one of these accounts is true either.

Fact or fiction?

Ghost investigators have to beware of such stories, in which warping elements of reckless repetition, of credulous endorsement, and of deliberate invention are at work. These factors hinder objective investigation and tend to throw a pall of doubt over ghost-hunting. But it is only fair to contrast the many accounts that appeal strictly on their own merits. Such accounts refer to unique events located at real places — by that token they are open to investigation, and over the years dedicated people have tried to unravel these enigmas to supply answers.

Yet dedication is not enough. Every would-be investigator is a product of his or her time and upbringing. Early education, with the possible introduction of fear-based teachings, can affect adult judgment and prejudice the understanding of strange, baffling events. It is no exaggeration to say that many who investigate ghosts have been rendered unsuitable for the task by fears, phantasms, cruel superstitions, and distorted values picked up in their vulnerable childhoods.

Enlightened attitude
Christoph Nicolai was a leader of the 18th-century German Enlightenment movement, as well as a bookseller and writer. In his late fifties he began to see apparitions. He refused, however, to believe that they had a ghostly source. He sought medical guidance and within months his hallucinations had ceased.

The late British psychic investigator Dr. Eric Dingwall (a ghost-hunter himself) used two extreme cases to illustrate the importance of one's frame of reference. He contrasted the visions of the 18th-century Swedish scientist and mystic Emanuel Swedenborg (1688–1772) with those of his contemporary, German writer Christoph Nicolai (1733–1811). At 55 Swedenborg began to see figures that filled him with awe. He interpreted them as angels and spirits, and from these encounters he imagined that he was being given the role of a messenger of God. His task was to unveil the spiritual sense of the Gospels for mankind, and indeed, he made this his life work, even though this involved terrifying battles with "evil spirits." At 57 Nicolai, too, began to see mysterious figures. Sometimes they were visions of the dead, at other times phantoms of the living.

Rational thinking
Unlike Swedenborg, Nicolai did not accept the visions unquestioningly as emissaries of God, but as aberrations due to ill health. His rationalist outlook led him to observe everything in detail and keep thorough records. His phantoms stopped appearing after three months, following a bloodletting session with leeches applied by his physician.

Nicolai published a famous paper on his ordeal. Swedenborg wrote many, much more famous works and founded the New Church, based on his visions. But, as Dr. Dingwall

> He interpreted them as angels and spirits, and from these encounters he imagined that he was being given the role of a messenger of God.

reminds us: "...the student of hallucinations will not forget the debt that is owed to Nicolai for bringing his case to the notice of the medical world." Swedenborg, on the other hand, writes of conversations with the inhabitants of Mars, Venus, and other planets. His religious yearnings seem finally to have overruled reality in favor of fantasy.

Logical landmarks
In the 18th and 19th centuries the landmark works of Daniel Defoe, *The Secrets of the Invisible World Disclos'd* (1735), and Catherine Crowe, *The Night Side of Nature* (1848), applied logic to the question of whether ghosts exist. But

Oppressive spirits
This drawing of "Antediluvian Spirits Pressing Down on My Head" by British artist John Flaxman (1755–1826), is based on text taken from Emanuel Swedenborg's major work, the Arcana Coelestia, *in which Swedenborg reported that when in his visionary state: "At a certain height above my head there were spirits, who flowed into my thoughts....They pressed down upon me with considerable force....I was informed that these spirits were those who lived before the flood."*

Swedenborg's vision of heaven
British artist William Blake (1757-1827) was a Swedenborgian, and his painting "The Last Judgment" is a depiction of Swedenborg's concept of God and heaven, based on his otherworldly visions.

after 1848 ghostly investigations fell under the sway of fantastic elements once again, with the expansion of the spiritualist movement.

Conversing with spirits

The teachings of the spiritualists affirmed that spirits of the dead were real. These spirits could speak through mediums, signal by raps and taps, and sometimes even make themselves visible. Various attempts to investigate these claims by the Dialectical Society in Britain, in 1869, were marred by an uncritical, indeed naive, attitude of trust. Many of the problems of mysterious materializations that could have been solved by proper investigation and rigorous searches of the venues, were left unresolved and treated as awesome puzzles. The society's report on "Spiritual Manifestations" was greeted by *The Times* as "nothing but a farrago of impotent conclusions, garnished by a mass of the most monstrous rubbish it has ever been our misfortune to sit in judgement upon."

In 1862 the Ghost Club, a society dedicated to the investigation of the paranormal, was founded in London. This was followed 20 years later by the British Society for Psychical Research (SPR), which was also founded in London. The SPR attempted to place fantasy to one side and declared its official purpose as "to examine without prejudice or prepossession and in a scientific spirit, those faculties of man, real or supposed, which appear to be inexplicable on any generally recognised hypothesis." One of its committees was set up to concentrate on haunted houses, and by 1886 the society had accumulated such a wealth of "testimony" from the general public that society founders Frederick Myers, Edmund Gurney, and Frank Podmore were able to produce their pioneering work, *Phantasms of the Living*.

But the SPR pioneers had their own problems. They were mainly intellectuals with high standards. The author, Renée Haynes, a senior member of the SPR, characterized them as "cool, detached, reasonable, lucid, scrupulously just and accurate in the pursuit of objective truth." This may have led them to underestimate or ignore the needs and drives in those eager to have their stories believed. It is doubtful that any of them understood how the search for self-esteem or personal recognition, could influence people's testimony. And they seriously undervalued the extent to which confused recall could be transmuted into fervent conviction.

Blind faith

An additional problem arose out of the SPR's early acceptance of telepathy as a proven reality. This complicated their attempts to understand the material offered to them. It is not surprising, then, to find that *Phantasms of the Living* ran into trouble before the glue had hardened on its bindings. It is "a meaningless collection of ghost stories," said Sir Oliver Lodge, who became president of the SPR in 1932. The Scottish skeptic, lawyer A. Taylor Innes, pointed out the bias in favor of telepathy and showed how this hindered the objective assessment of the evidence.

Later investigations by the SPR were of a higher standard, but fashions changed and the society became more interested in mediumship and its implications. Ghosts were neglected. Yet in the meantime there were plenty of societies, clubs, and individuals prepared to take on the task of ghost-hunting.

> It is not surprising to find that *Phantasms of the Living* ran into trouble before the glue had hardened on its bindings.

A new approach
British philosopher Edmund Gurney (1847–88) was a founding member of the Society for Psychical Research and, along with his investigative colleagues, he attempted to give ghostly research a more scientific basis.

THE GHOST CLUB

Membership is by invitation only and has included celebrities, writers, and mystics among its number. Despite numerous declines and revivals since its founding more than a century ago, the Ghost Club is still going strong.

Peter Underwood
The Ghost Club has flourished in recent years with the ghost investigator and author, Peter Underwood, as its president.

In 1862 TWO YOUNG MAGICIANS, the Davenport brothers, traveled from the United States to England. They never claimed to be spiritualist mediums, but then they never denied it either, and they proceeded to thrill London society with what appeared to be their amazing ability to make contact with the spirit world. But not everyone was taken in by the Davenport brothers' tricks, and a group of gentlemen interested in the ghost phenomenon got together to investigate the brothers, along with any other reports of ghostly contact. The group called themselves the Ghost Club, and the club's founding members included headmasters, clergymen, and academics. Other early members included such celebrities as Charles Dickens, W. B. Yeats, Sir Arthur Conan Doyle, and Sir Osbert Sitwell. Although the Ghost Club has undergone a number of closures and revivals over the years, it still exists today.

Male domain
The club's first revival took place in 1882, at the instigation of the Rev. Stainton Moses, a founding member of the British Society for Psychical Research. Women were excluded from membership, which was reserved for "clubbable men — gentlemen, to exclude all cranks and crotcheteers, and to meet on the first of each month as a social club." In 1936 the club closed down and its records were deposited at the British Museum in London. But within two years the renowned psychical researcher Harry Price had re-formed the club, admitting women to its ranks for the first time. This third incarnation was a convivial affair, meeting every six weeks for dinner to discuss all aspects of ghost-hunting and to hear about members' own experiences of the paranormal. Guest speakers would address such

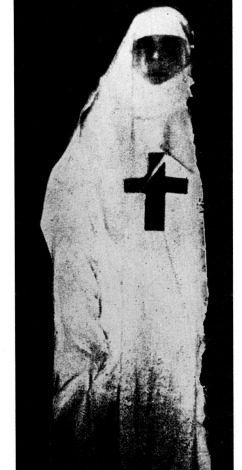

topics as clairvoyance, survival evidence, ghosts in fact and fiction, and "spirit" photographs, as well as exposing various fraudulent tricksters.

In 1947 Harry Price invited ghost-hunter Peter Underwood to join the club, but within a few months Price was dead and, leaderless, the club lost its impetus once again. But seven years later, the club became an active association once more, spurred on by Philip Paul, a spiritualist investigator (who was a member for a few months only in 1954) and Percival Seward, founder of the Association of Psychic Research Societies, and later chairman of the club.

Open debate
In 1960 Peter Underwood was elected president, and, since then, with the renowned writer on the paranormal, Colin Wilson, as vice-president, the club has flourished. It welcomes skeptics and believers alike and encourages open debate among its members. As Underwood explains: "The club is not tied in its approach to any given subject; one of its main objects is to discuss current psychic topics in an inquiring spirit."

Ghost photo?
The authenticity of "spirit" photographs has often been debated by members of the Ghost Club. This photograph supposedly shows the partial materialization of a nun, taken at a séance held at Lison, France, in 1918. It was dismissed as fraudulent following scrutiny by Ghost Club members.

THE INVESTIGATORS

Ghost-hunters come in many different guises: gullible believers, dramatic deceivers, and skeptical inquirers. Unfortunately, the most flamboyant and entertaining tend also to be more inclined toward ghost creation.

IRISHMAN ELLIOTT O'DONNELL (*c.* 1872–1965) was one of many gentlemen amateur ghost-hunters practicing in the early 20th century, and he was the first to admit that he did not employ a scientific approach. O'Donnell said of himself: "I lay no claim to being what is termed a scientific psychical researcher. I am not a member of any august society that conducts its investigations of the other world, or worlds, with test tube and weighing apparatus; neither do I pretend to be a medium or a consistent clairvoyant — I have never undertaken to 'raise' ghosts at will for the sensation-seeker or the tourist. I am merely a ghost-hunter. One

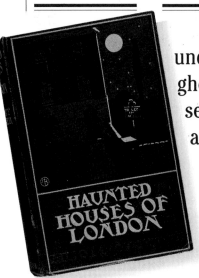

> "I have never undertaken to 'raise' ghosts at will for the sensation-seeker....I am merely a ghost-hunter. One who lays stake by his own eyes and senses."
>
> **Elliott O'Donnell**

who lays stake by his own eyes and senses; one who honestly believes that he inherits in some degree the faculty of psychic perceptiveness from a long line of Celtic ancestry; and who is, and always has been, deeply and genuinely interested in all questions relative to phantasms and a continuation of individual life after physical dissolution."

Such sincerity is quite disarming, but so is that antique tongue-sweetener known as blarney. In O'Donnell's world ghosts slobber, rant, rave, and hurl themselves about with murderous intent. His very first dangerous ghost actually gripped him by the throat with long clammy fingers, forced him down onto his bed, and choked him into a state of unconsciousness. Equally awe-inspiring was the phantom of the blue-eyed

footman whose hair was close-cropped, bristling, and orange. He leered, jeered, glided, and bounded. His murderous intentions were unmistakably signaled by the open razor he waved in his loathsome hairy hand. O'Donnell's most endearing ghost, though, must surely be the one said to haunt a house in Virginia. It was a disembodied human head with wide-open glaring eyes. It peered in through windows and peeped over banisters, eternally repeating one word: "Blood." But such collections of startling anecdotes and chilling reminiscences do not provide answers to serious questions.

Authentic tales?

Another popular author of ghostly tales, the late James Reynolds, also benefited from the blarney in his stories about Irish hauntings. Canadian-born Reynolds had an expert's knowledge of architecture and fine skills as an illustrator. His main investigations are found in his *Gallery of*

Reynolds insisted that he made his own thorough investigations of the places he wrote about.

Ghosts, Ghosts in Irish Houses, and *More Ghosts in Irish Houses.* Reynolds insisted that he made his own thorough investigations of the places he wrote about. He claimed he saw for himself and interviewed those who had first-hand experiences of the ghostly events he related. One of his most fascinating cases concerns the ghost of a great soprano and is found in his book *Ireland* (1953). The soprano case is of considerable interest, since, according to Reynolds, the singer's very solid-looking ghost was seen all over the world, in Vienna, Paris, London, Dublin, and often at her home in Kerry.

Overnight sensation

Reynolds explains that the ghostly soprano was one Stella Boynton, who was born in Portrush, County Antrim, in 1873. Her mother had been a singer with a minor traveling operatic company, and young Stella took to singing as if it were

111

destined. At the age of 15, she made her concert debut in Cork and "woke next morning to find herself the rage." In 1889 she began serious studies, first in Dublin, then London, then Rome. She made her professional debut at the Theatre Royal, Dublin, in August 1894, taking the role of Violetta in Verdi's *La Traviata*.

Spellbound czar

In 1899, Reynolds wrote that Boynton appeared in St. Petersburg before the czar, who told her that her voice had a magical quality that he had never heard before. Shortly after this triumph she married Capt. John Dunn of the Irish Fusiliers and went to live at his ancestral home, Cartymore Abbey. There, claimed Reynolds, she led a happy life, entertaining the local gentry and their ladies. Apparently she also bore her husband a son.

She still toured, and sang in Paris, Vienna, and Rome. Then in the summer of 1903 Stella began showing signs of paranoia. She accused her guests of spying on her and cut herself off from all her friends. It seems that she had been indulging in cocaine and morphine, and her thoughts were growing ever more morbid. The drugs eventually took over, and Stella Dunn disappeared from the abbey some time in October 1903

Captain Dunn was baffled and frantic, without a lead to follow. And then he read a fantastic item in a London newspaper. It said: "Late yesterday afternoon a disturbance was caused by a woman outside the Albert Hall. She wore a grass-green cape and a large green hat....As she was being led away for questioning, she shouted that she had an engagement to sing at the Albert Hall, she had sung there many times. She must sing, she shrieked, 'Sing for my Supper.'"

The report went on to say that the unidentified woman had been arrested and charged with vagrancy. John Dunn, though, had no doubts about her identity, and he left at once for London and a reunion with his wife. But as he stepped from the Holyhead Express at Euston Station, he saw the heart-stopping newspaper headline: "Woman in Green murdered in Soho." The police took Dunn to the morgue and there he identified his wife's body — she had been strangled.

She had broken away from the matron in charge of the women's remand quarters and was next found dead in a Soho lodging house. It was a killing without clues or recognizable motives. Stella Dunn was buried in the crypt at Cartymore alongside the other members of the Dunn family. The house was closed and the broken-hearted Captain Dunn rejoined his regiment in India.

Ghostly appearances

Six months later, according to James Reynolds, Stella Dunn's ghost appeared at the abbey. It stood by the drawing room piano and silently mouthed the words of a song. Then an old friend, Mr. Caruthers, swore that Stella's ghost had sat at his table in a café in Vienna. She was apparently seen in Paris. And a Mrs. Ardlin told Reynolds that she had seen Stella twice while staying at the abbey with Stella's grandson O'More Dunn. Reynolds himself even fancied that he saw her ghost on Dublin's Grafton Street — though he couldn't swear to it. Still that didn't matter too much, for many other sober witnesses testified to the existence of the phantom "woman in green."

This investigation by James Reynolds was so masterly in its details that three English investigators working for a British television company decided to follow up the hauntings and bring the story up to

> **According to James Reynolds, Dunn's ghost appeared at the abbey. It stood by the drawing room piano and silently mouthed the words of a song.**

Bogus beauty
Author James Reynolds drew this likeness of the opera singer Stella Dunn to illustrate his book, Ireland. *However, extensive investigation has proved that Dunn never existed.*

date. In 1990 they commissioned an experienced researcher living in County Cork and asked him to set up a visit to the abbey. His response was startling. He had contacted post offices, libraries, and local history groups in the Kerry area, but no one had ever heard of Cartymore Abbey — yet, according to Reynolds, the place was still being used by the Dunn family when he wrote his book in 1953. No newspaper reports could be found alluding to the 1888 concert debut in Cork, even though Reynolds claimed that he had seen the accounts in print. As for the murder in Soho, this was not mentioned in any newspaper column or any police records covering the month of October 1903.

Further checks showed that no opera house in the world had ever heard of this "great soprano." In fact, the only Irish soprano to achieve international fame was Margaret Burke Sheridan, who died peacefully in the 1950's. And the only Irish soprano with a remotely similar name is Veronica Dunne, who still teaches in Dublin. The memorable

abbey, the murder, the victim, and the hauntings, were all pure invention.

Poised between sensationalists such as Elliott O'Donnell and James Reynolds and worthy rationalists such as the British Society for Psychical Research (SPR) lies the man considered by many to be the greatest of the ghost-hunters — the enigmatic Harry Price. By the time of his death in March 1948, Price was the most renowned investigator of all. His was the name that inevitably came up when ghosts and hauntings were discussed. Harry Price was an intriguing mixture of dedication and self-promotion, and he put enormous amounts of both time and energy into his investigations into the para-normal, which began in earnest in 1920.

Borley Rectory

Price's most notorious investigation involved "the most haunted house in England" — Borley Rectory. The story begins in June 1929 when Price received a telephone call from the highly excited editor of the *Daily Mirror* in London.

According to the newspaper, the story involved "ghostly figures of headless coachmen and a nun, an old-time coach drawn by two bay horses, which appears and vanishes mysteriously, and dragging footsteps in empty rooms." All of these things were apparently happening at a rectory situated a few miles away from Long Melford, in Suffolk.

Before Price set foot in the place, there were numerous reports of things

> **The story involved "ghostly figures of headless coachmen and a nun, an old-time coach drawn by two bay horses, which appears and vanishes mysteriously...."**

Ghost trap
As part of his investigation of a haunted house, Harry Price used vases as "controls." Price ringed the vases with chalk marks so that he could see if any force had moved them in his absence.

Authentic performer
Margaret Burke Sheridan (1889–1958) was the only Irish opera soprano to achieve international fame. Her birth date coincides with the start of Stella Dunn's career, and her professional achievements match Dunn's exactly. It seems likely that author James Reynolds borrowed Sheridan's history and gave it to his fictional creation, Stella Dunn.

seen and heard. Within days of Price's arrival at the house the phenomena became more violent. Apparently, a piece of brick smashed a window, a red glass candlestick was hurled down the main staircase, a mothball hit an assistant on the hand, and a cascade of pebbles came tumbling down the stairs. When house bells began ringing of their own accord and two keys fell out of their locks at the same time, this was the signal for Price to call for a séance.

At 1 A.M. six people assembled in the Blue Room, with Price very much in

Front-page news
Stella Cranshaw (right) predicted that an advertisement for Andrews Liver Salt (below) would appear on the cover of the Daily Mail *on May 19, 1923. It transpired that information regarding the cover was already available when she made her forecast.*

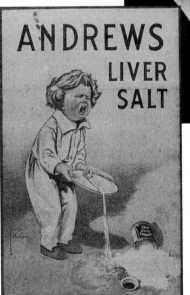

charge. The six included the resident vicar, Rev. G. E. Smith, and his wife, and two sisters of the late Rev. Harry Bull, the previous resident. Price addressed the four walls of the room with the plea: "If any entity is present here tonight, will it please make itself known."

After three such appeals, Price claimed, the tapping began. It was quickly found to be coming from the wooden back of a dressing-table mirror. By using the time-honored three taps for "yes," one tap for "no," it was speedily established that the presence was the late rector, Reverend Bull. Apparently it was his footsteps that were heard around the house. So began the

lengthy and convoluted saga of the Borley investigation. Its confused and complex history has been recorded in a number of books and scores of articles. When he died in 1948, Price was even planning to issue yet another book on the hauntings. But after his death, examination of his unpublished notes and correspondence showed that the case that had brought him world renown had been so distorted that it is doubtful if the truth can ever be fully known. And there is some evidence that Price was willing to tamper with results when it suited him.

This tampering was apparently not restricted to the Borley affair. There is, for example, some controversy over the famous sitting of April 12, 1923, at which Price's favorite medium, Stella Cranshaw, was said to have accurately forecast the

> ## "If any entity is present here tonight, will it please make itself known." After three such appeals, Price claimed, the tapping began.

front page of the *Daily Mail* 37 days in advance of publication (May 19, 1923). Clairvoyantly she attempted to describe a new advertisement for Andrews Liver Salt. The match between her words and the printed picture was uncanny.

A suspect claim

Price's biographer, Paul Tabori, states: "Harry Price took immediate steps to investigate the circumstances of this strange event. The Andrews people told him that they had prepared the advertisement after the date of the séance." But in Price's correspondence files at London University there is a letter that shows this claim to be suspect. The letter is to Price from the managing director of Scott & Turner, the makers of Andrews Liver Salt. It states unequivocally that their advertisement was in London before the date of the séance and the knowledge of its existence was "shared by several people." By concealing these facts, Harry Price left himself open to accusations of

▶ PAGE 116

ACADEMIC ATTITUDES

Sadly, academics often lower their standards when faced with the intriguing world of ghosts, and myths and misconceptions are constantly being given a false aura of respectability.

N APRIL 1987 the Parapsychology Foundation at Athens State College in Alabama publicized a concert that was to be staged on May 12 at the college's McCandless Hall in memory of the operatic soprano Abigail Lylia Burns. There was a well-known legend that Burns had died in a tragic accident in 1914 shortly after performing at the auditorium.

According to the parapsychologists, her ghost began to haunt the auditorium soon afterward. "Deep into the winter following her death," they said, "a ghostly image of a young woman, her golden hair glistening in the moonlight, was sighted at the third-floor window of McCandless Hall. She wore a white gown and at her breast she clutched a bouquet of red roses. Through the years, the sightings continued."

Spiritual expectations

The memorial concert, which was organized by Dr. Joe Slate, chairman of the college's division of behavioral sciences, gained wide publicity and attracted hundreds of people hoping to catch a glimpse of the phantom. Of these eager hopefuls, however, only three reported anything paranormal. One witness, soprano Helen Matsos, who was onstage, said she had felt Abigail's presence. Another witness, Ed Langla, a past-life hypnotherapist, said he saw her wave goodbye, "for the purpose of the evening was to let Abigail transcend to the place she needed to go." The third witness, Naoko Worrell, reported that he had heard the ghost. "Every time the soprano sings," he said, "Abigail sings along."

A small group of students in the audience believed that these reports were due to people at the concert having been conditioned to expect a paranormal event. Seven of them approached Mark W. Durm, associate professor of psychology, to propose researching Abigail's history. Their findings were striking.

After checking the historical records of Athens State college, the county archives, and the 1914 issues of the local newspapers, they could find no trace of Abigail's alleged visit in 1914 and no record of the concert. No trace could be found, either, of Abigail Burns herself. A request for her

Table-tilting
Dr. Joe Slate looks on as his students attempt to contact the ghost of singer Abigail Burns.

death certificate produced this statement from the state registrar: "No record was found to exist of the death of Abigail Lylia Burns during 1908–1922 in Limestone/Madison County, Alabama."

How then did the foundation come to claim that Abigail's ghost was one of the more widely known paranormal occurrences in northern Alabama? The answer is supplied by a local newspaper, the *Decatur Daily* for May 12, 1987, which reports: "Many of the details of Miss Burns surfaced through techniques used by the parapsychology classes. Through table-tilting, in which a spirit can communicate with this world by causing the table to tilt in response to questions, the class learned that a heartbroken lover of Miss Burns would frequent their former meeting place on the third floor of McCandless Hall after her death because he felt close to her there."

Professor's explanation

Professor Durm explains the parapsychologists' persistent faith in the May 12 appearance: "It was a perfect example of cognitive bias. Selective perception and selective exposure had caused reason to sleep, and as the adage warns, 'The sleep of reason brings forth monsters.' In this case, the monster was a golden-haired, white-cloaked singer. But in seven seeking students, reason had not slept."

THE DECATUR DAILY

Decatur takes area tournament victory
Sports/C1

76th YEAR—No. 57

"My country, may she ever be right, but, right or wrong, my country" — COMMODORE STEPHEN DECATUR

DECATUR, ALABAMA 35601, THURSDAY, APRIL 23, 1987

CITY EDITION

36 PAGES

Skeptics: Opera singer, ghost never existed

By ELIZABETH ANDERSON
DAILY Staff Writer

ATHENS — Will the ghost of Abigail Burns appear tonight at Athens State College when the Huntsville Opera Theater performs in McCandless Hall?

Members of Dr. Mark Durm's skeptical thinking class say "No" because they believe she never existed.

They claim to have debunked the story of a young opera singer who performed in McCandless Hall in 1914 and has haunted the place since her death that night while en route to her next engagement in Huntsville.

The Huntsville group will perform at 7:30 p.m. selections by Verdi including "La Traviata."

Members of the eight-member skeptical thinking class, which includes James Limbach, Lea Terry and Rhonda Garrett, said they spent 20 to 50 hours this quarter trying to find a record of the woman, but to no avail.

They went through hundreds of newspaper pages in Limestone County and Huntsville looking for a mention of the concert or the woman's fatal carriage accident later that night, but found none.

According to Durm, an associate professor of psychology who says he does not believe in ghosts, neither the Alabama Courier found...

"They were the only two newspapers in existence in Limestone County at the time. Both papers were so cognizant of events at the college and reported very trivial matter that occurred at the college, yet nowhere was the announcement of Abigail Lylia Burns' concert stated," said Durm.

The only opera singer among the six was Enrico Arsoni, "a well-known dramatic tenor," according to the Alabama Courier.

Legend has it that the beech tree on the north side of McCandless Hall was planted in honor of Miss Burns...

know for sure was to ask Marg... tree. They decided against tha... The class also asked Marg... who attended the college in... and she said she never hear... story.

THE GHOST DETECTOR

John Cutten, a former secretary of the SPR, devised a portable apparatus for taking to "haunted houses." It consists of a main control box containing the electronics; a camera loaded with infrared film; a wind vane; an ordinary camera controlling a flash unit; a flash unit with infrared filter; a tape recorder; a vibrator under the wind vane; a triggering apparatus for the infrared camera; a bulb for remote control of the camera; a photoelectric cell; a microphone; a pilot light and a thermostatic control.

Unproven apparatus

Cutten's "Ghost Hunter" was devised to detect drafts of air, vibrations, changes in illumination, noises, changes in temperature, and physical disturbances. Any major changes in a room cause the unit to operate automatically. Camera 1 takes a photo with the infrared film at the same time as a buzzer sounds to wake up any sleeping investigators, and the tape recorder switches on.

This apparatus has been shown on a number of television programs in Britain, Japan, Spain, and the U.S.A. But does it work? Mr. Cutten dryly stated: "So far it has been triggered once only when a vase was found broken on a floor, presumably knocked off the shelf by the cat, which was also in the room!"

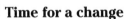
John Cutten's ghost detector

deception. But why did he allow himself to become party to such a lie?

Perhaps the best insight into Price's personality is provided by British researcher Dr. Eric Dingwall, who wrote: "Mr. Price's real interest was not in science but in publicity....It is only by realizing Harry Price's excusable love of the limelight and of personal adulation that we can understand his work....The unequalled opportunities that came his way were not used for the purposes of scientific research, but in order to forward the personal interests and ambitions that dominated his life." Yet Dr. Dingwall does admit that through Mr. Price's numerous articles and books the general public learnt a great deal about mediums, haunted houses, and other paranormal phenomena.

Time for a change

Up until the 1950's, investigations were usually conducted by those already dedicated to a belief in a paranormal basis for ghosts and hauntings. It became clear that a new, more rational approach to ghost-hunting would have to be adopted. The New Zealander Andrew MacKenzie was one of the first of a new breed of investigator. MacKenzie was a journalist by profession and his interest in ghost-hunting began in 1960 when he was asked to write a series of articles on ghosts.

Since then he has become heavily involved with the work of the British SPR, and has investigated many ghostly reports. MacKenzie has little faith in impressions

Ghost-hunter Andrew MacKenzie

from psychics at the scene of a haunting, nor does he use any kind of ghostbusting equipment. He believes that his old-fashioned journalistic methods of double-checking all facts and sources and never taking anything for granted are invaluable in his research, and he is adamant that a natural explanation should always be sought before a paranormal one is assumed. This refreshingly new, unbiased attitude was also shared by the late American investigator into the paranormal, D. Scott Rogo (1950–90).

Media personality

Even more recently the American investigator Prof. Hans Holzer has received much public attention following numerous TV and radio appearances. His publisher states that he is the author of more than 81 books, including: *Yankee Ghosts*, *Ghosts I've Met*, *The Lively Ghosts of Ireland*, *Gothic Ghosts*, *The Phantoms of Dixie*, and *Ghosts of the Golden West*. Unlike Andrew MacKenzie, Professor Holzer favors the use of a medium, who visits the sites of hauntings with him and recites her psychic knowledge about the places, the people, and the past history as it unfolds in her mind. He has applied this technique to such events as Booth's role in the killing of Lincoln, and other well-known tragedies. The result is then worked up into book form.

Worthwhile conclusions

It appears that as long as people tell ghost stories there will be individuals with extremely varied attitudes who will want to investigate them. But the future of ghost-hunting clearly demands that, whenever a case emerges, there is cooperation between skeptics and paranormalists. Only in this way, with neither side having a privileged position, can worthwhile conclusions be reached.

CASEBOOK
A HAUNTING IN ALAMEDA

"Based on what we heard about the experiences, the 'behavior' of the phenomena, and the history of the house, we concluded that this was a haunting...."

IN 1989 GHOST-HUNTER Loyd Auerbach and his partner, Christopher Chacon, set up the Office of Paranormal Investigations in Orinda, California, manned by a staff of 12 investigators. In 1991 Auerbach and his team looked into the case of a reported ghostly presence in a house in Alameda. The following account was compiled by Loyd Auerbach himself:

"A family of four, a mother whom we'll call Nancy and her three children (in their teen and pre-teen years), had moved into a rented house in Alameda a few months before. Nancy called to report strange goings-on in the house.

Face in the closet

"What Nancy and the children experienced were phenomena of various types. Nancy 'felt' the presence of an 'old lady' almost from the time they moved in. Her daughter reported seeing an 'old lady' coming down the stairs from the attic. The sighting of the elderly woman continued, and was seen by Nancy, a friend of hers, and her sons. Nancy also saw a face in the closet, though not that of the same old woman.

Childhood memories

"Their landlord was himself apparently a problem in that he just couldn't seem to stay away from his childhood home (he even left clothing, furniture, and knick-knacks when he rented it out). He and his brother had been adopted, and from what the landlord told them, Nancy got the impression that his stepmother was a 'taskmaster,' that the 'old lady' they saw was the landlord's mother, and that everything somehow related to her.

"My team and I came into this case with few preconceptions. First, before any more information than I knew was passed on to the team, I had them walk around for their impressions. They were to mark off any places on a floor plan to see if they 'felt' anything in certain spots.

"After hearing the descriptions of the experiences and the phenomena, we interviewed the family members and were able to add experiences to what they had first offered. The spots marked off by the team members seemed to match very closely with the spots where the reported incidents seemed to occur.

Sources of magnetism

"We then walked around the house using a magnetic scanner, charting any fluctuations in magnetic fields in the house (including those that come from appliances, TV's, and even light fixtures and wiring). We expected to find higher readings near the electrical devices. However, what was most interesting was that the places with the higher than average readings of magnetism also correlated to the places where the family reported the events.

"Based on what we heard about the experiences, the 'behavior' of the phenomena, and the history of the house, we concluded that this was a haunting, that somehow the family members were perceiving bits of information relating to what had gone on in the house over time, sort of recorded snatches of history.

"Since there seemed to be some sort of connection between the past history of the house and the phenomena, we suggested any remodelling work be speeded up. As the changes took place (from repainting to getting the landlord's belongings out), so did the experiences subside. It was as though Nancy and her family had succeeded in 'recording over' the old memories."

DETECTOR ON CALL

How exactly do investigators of the paranormal go about their business? Loyd Auerbach, who holds a masters degree in parapsychology, and who has his own ghostbusting company in California, gives a detailed rundown of the procedure.

"CONTRARY TO POPULAR BELIEF," says Loyd Auerbach, "those of us who investigate reports of apparitions, hauntings, and poltergeists, or other paranormal phenomena, do *not* walk into any situation assuming we will find something for sure. We don't rely on psychics to investigate. We don't conduct exorcisms. And we certainly don't carry the kinds of gizmos the ghostbusters did in the films.

Angled approach

"Parapsychologists and investigators of the paranormal look at the experiences from two basic angles. Many move into a situation, attempt to ascertain what may really be happening, paranormal or not, and then attempt to collect data to add to the knowledge base of the field. Others have the concerns of those reporting the situations uppermost in their minds, the well-being of the people taking precedence over any data gathering. Some of us try to do both."

Auerbach says that a typical case begins with a phone call. An individual, after searching for someone to talk to, finally "finds" a parapsychologist or reputable investigator. The investigator makes an initial assessment of the situation based on the conversation with the caller, then considers several aspects of the case before agreeing to a visit.

First, he needs to ascertain if this is the kind of case he can deal with. For example, Auerbach's company refers UFO cases to others, since they do not conduct UFO investigations. Sometimes a report may sound too much like a horror film to be worth taking on, and sometimes it seems likely that the call is a hoax.

Normal explanations

Secondly, the investigator needs to decide if there are any immediately identifiable "normal" explanations. "The questions asked should be directed at learning about the caller's background as well as about the physical environment," explains Auerbach. "For example, a house where things vibrate on the wall may be located on a street with heavy traffic. It is important to eliminate any other explanations, whether they are paranormal or psychological. If we don't do that, then any data gathering may yield a lot of false information about the case we're attempting to study." Multiple-witness cases yield more information, so it is helpful to speak to as many people as possible. They help assess the possible paranormality of a situation and give useful insight into how the people deal with the unusual occurrences they are experiencing.

"Finally," says Auerbach, "there is timing. If the experience occurred only once, be it yesterday or 10 years ago, we might only be able to guess as to what happened. If it is a repeated experience, it is more interesting. If it is currently occurring, it is more open to investigation.

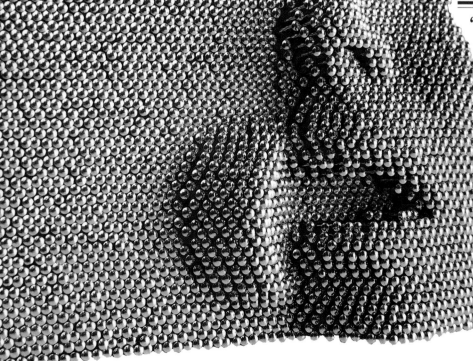

> "The investigator weighs each little piece of information against both possible normal explanations and the knowledge base of parapsychology."

"Good paranormal investigators are a careful lot. It does no one any good to go blindly into a situation assuming things are just as the witnesses said. Weeding out the potentially paranormal cases is a time-saver for both investigator and witness.

"Most people find the phenomena unnerving. So whether they have really seen a ghost or not, once they think they have, sounds of the house settling or the unexpected breeze from the doorway, for example, are immediately deemed paranormal too.

They may decide to leave well enough alone, or they may decide they want the phenomena stopped, the ghost gone.

"During an investigation," continues Auerbach, "the investigator interviews the witnesses, and attempts to ascertain both the timing of the events and where they all occurred. The investigator weighs each little piece of information against both possible normal explanations and the knowledge base of parapsychology to ascertain if the case is paranormal or not."

Confirmation of events

Once the investigator has determined that something of a paranormal nature is occurring, says Auerbach, he may use some of the tools of the trade to collect more data or to try to confirm some facets of the experiences. Trying to prove the existence of the phenomena is not yet an option. He will merely attempt to provide the witnesses with information as to what might be going on and impart some basic parapsychological data.

What comes next is often up to the witnesses themselves. Since they are now armed with a better understanding of what may be going on, they are in a position to decide what they want done. They may decide to leave well enough alone, or they may decide they want the phenomena stopped, the ghost gone.

In the latter case, the investigator may do one or all of several things. He may suggest books to read or techniques to try that have been successful in removing spirits in the past. Since there is no one but the witnesses to vouch for the phenomena, the success of these techniques is subjective.

Psychological viewpoint

The investigator may refer the witnesses to a humanistic or transpersonal counselor. If a witness believes that he or she has seen a ghost, he or she may need to deal with the emotional and psychological ramifications of the experience, perhaps by going to see a psychologist. On some occasions the referral may be to someone as mundane as a building contractor or an electrician or a plumber or even a real estate agent.

"Whether people do see ghosts is currently unprovable from an objective, scientific perspective," concludes Auerbach, "but then, so is the existence of the human mind. Some of the phenomena do, however, provide physical, observable effects, so whether they are objective or not, the investigator is there to help his clients to understand what the experiences might mean. He is also concerned with learning more himself, in order to gain a better understanding of the paranormal."

INVESTIGATING EQUIPMENT

A competent ghostbuster will use certain devices to ascertain the truth or otherwise of a reported paranormal happening:

◆ Recording equipment: Recording devices are used to record the testimony of witnesses and progress of the investigators. Audio recorders, 35mm still cameras, and video cameras are often used. Infrared imaging equipment is rarely used, as it seems to yield little.

◆ Environmental recording equipment: Under special circumstances, investigators need to use devices to check and record environmental conditions, such as temperature, humidity, air pressure, and so on. These help to monitor the physical environment, as well as keep track of any changes that may occur.

◆ Environmental tracking devices: Investigators now use hand-held magnetic scanners to look for correlations between high (and often unusual) magnetic fields and the locations where phenomena were reported. In cases where physical movement is said to have occurred, investigators may be able to use motion detectors and surveillance cameras.

◆ Use of people: Not surprisingly, investigators often make use of people who claim to have psychic abilities to see if what they "pick up" confirms and possibly adds to what has been reported. Investigators may also use a control group of people unrelated to the case (perhaps consisting of some "believers," some "skeptics") to see if they can also "pick up" what is reported without being prompted in any way.

CHAPTER SIX

IN SEARCH OF AN ANSWER

For thousands of years people have reported seeing ghosts of one kind or another. Psychical researchers have investigated the phenomenon in depth. Yet despite the wealth of accounts, research, and debate, no one can say with certainty whether ghosts exist or not!

Some of us may be prepared to accept the possibility that certain ghost stories might be genuine. Yet few of those who take this position would be willing to pronounce definitely on what the exact nature of such experiences might be. Are they purely subjective — that is, do the apparitions some claim to have seen exist only in the mind of the beholder? Or might ghost-sightings involve perceptions of entities that actually exist in the physical world?

All an illusion?

Extreme skeptics, of course, believe that all ghost sightings are nothing more than fancies or visual illusions, triggered, for example, by a trick of the light, a misperception of an ordinary object, or a degree of physical illness or damage, such as a fever or stroke. It may indeed be true that such circumstances might be responsible for some ghost sightings, but the theory does not provide a blanket explanation for all sightings, because many ghosts are seen in good light, when there is little chance of an optical illusion occurring, and while the witness is apparently in a normal, healthy mental state.

Storytelling?

Skeptics also question the veracity of witnesses' ghost-sighting accounts. And it is true that, because ghost stories are popular, the temptation to invent one, or to embellish one based on what was little more than a vague, doubtful experience, might be strong in some people. Or a witness might not deliberately fabricate, but simply misinterpret his or her experience at a later date. If this is the case, how, the skeptics demand, can we place any reliance on any witnesses' accounts?

Telling details

However, in a great many well-documented cases, a witness has given a clear, detailed, and convincing description of his or her experience and done this with another person at the time of the event or immediately

Masked mediums
Members of the Egungun Society, from the Yoruba tribe of southwestern Nigeria, appear at ceremonies in painted wood masks like this one, to convey messages from dead ancestors to their living descendants.

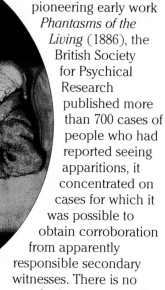

A Christmas Carol
In this classic ghost story by Charles Dickens, the miserly Scrooge is visited by a number of ghosts offering advice and warnings. This illustration by Arthur Rackham depicts the phantom of Scrooge's former partner berating the miser.

after it. When, in its pioneering early work *Phantasms of the Living* (1886), the British Society for Psychical Research published more than 700 cases of people who had reported seeing apparitions, it concentrated on cases for which it was possible to obtain corroboration from apparently responsible secondary witnesses. There is no proof, of course, that all were telling the truth, yet it would be equally unreasonable to suppose that all, or even most, of the witnesses were lying.

Coincidence?

The all-in-the-mind theory has another drawback. It fails to account for what are known as crisis apparitions, instances in which the witness sees the

> **Many ghosts are seen in good light, when there is little chance of an optical illusion occurring, and while the witness is apparently in a normal, healthy mental state.**

ghost of a person known to him or her at exactly or close to the time when, in another place, that person is dying or undergoing some other crisis. Such apparitions might be explained away, perhaps as due to a combination of over-heated imagination and coincidence. Yet in many cases, the witness describes the critical event in great detail, and his or her account is later verified.

Those who believe in the objective existence of ghosts, however, have to

▶ PAGE 124

CHURCHYARD PHANTOM

"I then saw Mrs. de Fréville leaning on the rails, dressed much as I had usually seen her....I slightly stumbled....When I looked up she was gone."

ON THE EVENING OF FRIDAY, MAY 8, 1885, Alfred Bard, a gardener who lived in Hinxton, England, was walking home from the village of Sawston, where he worked. As usual, he passed through the churchyard in Hinxton. At about 9:20 P.M., as he claimed later (in an account published in 1886 by the British Society for Psychical Research in *Phantasms of the Living*), he saw the figure of a former employer, Mrs. de Fréville. At the time, he had every reason to believe that she was alive and well.

"On entering the churchyard, I looked rather carefully at the ground....In so doing, I looked straight at the square stone vault in which the late Mr. de Fréville was at one time buried. I then saw Mrs. de Fréville leaning on the rails, dressed much as I had usually seen her, in a coal-scuttle bonnet, black jacket...and black dress. She was looking full at me."

Although Alfred Bard noticed that Mrs. de Fréville looked very pale, he was not particularly surprised to see her, as he "supposed she had come, as she sometimes did, to the mausoleum in her own park, in order to have it opened and go in."

"She was gone"
Bard's account continues: "I walked round the tomb, looking carefully at it, in order to see if the gate was open, keeping my eye on her and never more than five or six yards from her. Her face turned and followed me. I passed between the church and the tomb (there are about four yards between the two) and peered forward to see whether the tomb was open....I slightly stumbled on a hassock of grass, and looked at my feet for a moment only. When I looked up she was gone."

Bard thought that Mrs. de Fréville had entered the tomb, but when he went to investigate, he was surprised to find the gate locked. He was then "much startled," and hurried home.

Death discovered
The next day, news reached Hinxton that Mrs. de Fréville had died in London the previous afternoon. When the Reverend C. T. Forster, vicar of Hinxton, heard of Bard's reported sighting of Mrs. de Fréville, he interviewed the gardener and reported the incident to the

Society for Psychical Research. Bard swore he had not known that Mrs. de Fréville had been seriously ill, and the vicar testified to the sobriety and character of the gardener: "He is a man of great observation, being a self-taught naturalist, and I am quite satisfied that he desires to speak the truth without any exaggeration." Bard himself stated: "I have never had any other hallucinations."

Some people might like to explain away such an apparently significant sighting by suggesting that it was merely a coincidence. But the story is compelling, especially as it involves seeing the ghost of a person, not known to be ill, on the very day she died.

"A Winter Night's Tale"
A painting by Irish artist Daniel Maclise (1806–70) that depicts a Victorian household listening to what appears to be a ghost story.

TELLING TALES

In numerous cultures around the world, the tradition of oral storytelling has been handed down from generation to generation. And before the advent of radio, movies, and television, the telling of tales was a principal form of family entertainment. Ghost stories, in particular, were often told by the fireside, especially at Christmas.

Curiosity and apprehension

The hold that ghost stories have always exerted on the popular imagination is an illustration of man's perennial interest in the possibility of a spirit world, an interest born of natural curiosity and apprehension about the unknown. Some people's fascination with the subject exists to an abnormal degree, and it may be that such persons are particularly predisposed to seeing ghosts.

face just as many objections to their hypotheses as those of a skeptical nature do to theirs. For example, almost all believers in the supernatural regard ghosts as the spirits of dead people or animals, spirits that have come back to earth with possibly benevolent or malevolent intent. But, of course, this is all speculation, for we do not know whether we survive death or not, nor, if we do survive, in what form we might continue to exist.

Ghost trains

This hypothesis also does nothing to explain why many reported phantoms have appeared in the form of living people, of animals, and of inanimate objects, such as trains and ships.

Why, if we each possess a spirit that is capable of returning to earth in spectral form after our death, do apparently so few spirits return? Why is the world not inundated with the ghosts of its former inhabitants?

Evil spirits

Another hypothesis put forward by some believers is that ghosts are in fact mischievous or evil spirits — or even the devil himself — that assume a human likeness to fool us. Yet another theory, in this case to explain apparitions of

Forces of evil
This painting, part of an altarpiece by Matthias Grünewald (c.1455–1528), depicts demons, or evil spirits, armed with sticks. One theory holds that ghosts are evil spirits who have taken on human likeness.

the living, is that we each have an astral self that can detach itself from our physical, earthbound body and appear in another place. These, too, are speculations for which there is no more proof than for any other hypothesis.

Why, if we each possess a spirit capable of returning to earth after our death, do apparently so few spirits return? Why is the world not inundated with the ghosts of its former inhabitants?

In this chapter we shall be looking in greater detail at the evidence for and against the "subjective" and "objective" theories about the existence of ghosts.

THE ARCHETYPAL GHOST

Only a small percentage of the population claims to have seen a ghost, and few admit to believing in ghosts — but there seems to be some consensus of opinion as to what they might look like.

THE POPULAR IMAGE OF A GHOST is a white, ephemeral figure floating some inches above the ground and perhaps uttering low moans. The substance of this perception was strikingly demonstrated by Mrs. Anna Sciagal, of Riga, Latvia. One night in 1934, while she was alone in the house, she heard thieves on the ground floor. Mrs. Sciagal wrapped herself in a sheet, and moved to the top of the stairs to await the intruders. According to the Italian magazine *Illustrazione del Popolo*, when the burglars' lamp revealed her sinister figure above them, one fled in terror while the other had a heart attack!

A tall, white figure

Another case of someone seeing a traditional representation of a ghost had an even more tragic ending. During the winter of 1804, reports of a tall, white figure emerging from a cemetery in the Hammersmith area of London, England, and attempting to accost passersby, grew into a sensational news item. According to Peter Haining's *A Dictionary of Ghosts* (1982), one woman even died of fright after spotting the terrifying apparition.

Ghostbusters

When local people became afraid to go out at night, a vigilante committee of self-appointed ghostbusters decided to try to catch the supposed phantom. For three nights they hid in the cemetery, seeing nothing. Then, on the fourth, they saw a white figure in the darkness. A shot was fired, and the apparition, in a most unghostly manner, fell to the ground. Rushing up to the body, the vigilantes found it was Thomas Milwood, a bricklayer, returning home from work in his cement-powdered clothes.

In view of these stories, it takes a brave man to dress up like a ghost to see how people might react, but in

Burglar alarm
With great presence of mind, Mrs. Sciagal disguised herself as a ghost to frighten away thieves.

Hammersmith haunting
A Victorian lantern slide showing the alleged Hammersmith ghost.

1959, Tony Cornell, a member of the Council of the Society for Psychical Research in Britain, did just that.

His findings were published in the Society's *Journal* in December 1960. His first experiment began at 10 P.M. on May 26, 1960, in the cemetery of St. Peter's Church, Castle Hill, Cambridge. "The church and graveyard are situated immediately next to the main road, which is lit by sodium lamps," explained Cornell. "Two undergraduate observers assisted me in the experiment...we draped over my head 12 feet of butter muslin so that it hung loosely from head to foot. Dressed in this manner I stood...leaning against a tree on the edge of the churchyard, 8 feet from the roadway and about 6 feet above the level of the road."

Disappointing results

The experiment lasted 20 minutes. Cornell spent approximately half his time wandering among the trees, and half standing motionless. During this time, some 90 vehicles, 40 cyclists, and 12 pedestrians passed the area — but only four of these passersby gave any sign of seeing the ghost, and only one of them took it upon himself to investigate the incident. This was a young man, who leaned over the fence and asked the "ghost" what it thought it was doing.

The results of two further experiments, conducted under similar conditions but in different locations, were equally disappointing. Cornell sadly concluded: "The results tend to...suggest that no matter how many experiments of this nature are undertaken, unless the percipient has at that time some psychological preconcept to see something paranormal he would not mistake an imitation for the real thing."

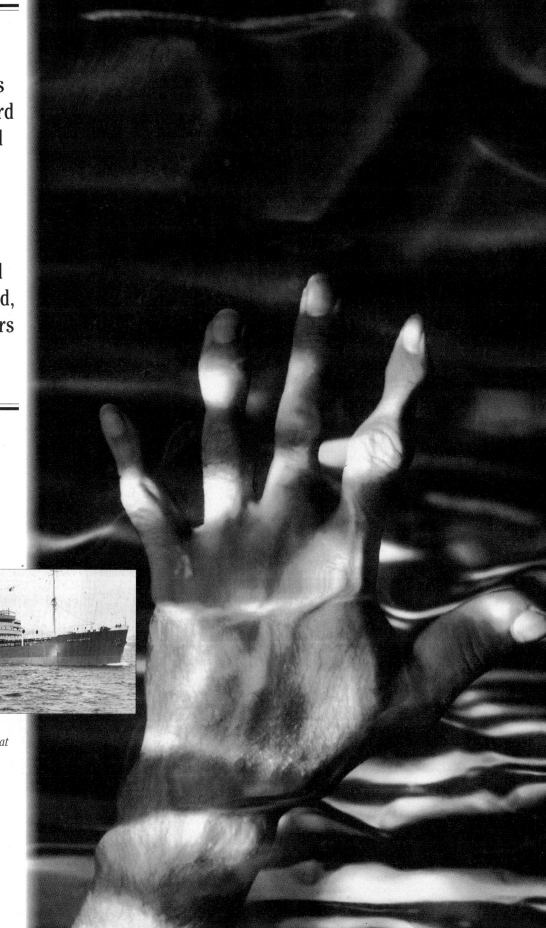

He saw two shipmates walking across the water toward him. They told him that if he swam toward the moon he would reach safety. He did as they directed, and a few hours later he was picked up....

Rescue boat
British Surveyor, *the tanker that picked up Arne Nicolaysen.*

In Time of Stress

A sailor overboard, alone in the ocean...climbers on Everest, gasping for oxygen...a family racked by collective guilt....Were the apparitions they saw inexplicably real or simply hallucinations, conjured up by people at the farthest extreme of stress?

O
N CHRISTMAS EVE 1955, in the Gulf of Mexico, Arne Nicolaysen, a Norwegian sailor, fell overboard from the deck of his ship *Hoegh Silver Spray*. No one saw him fall, and his ship steamed away in the dark without him. For many hours Nicolaysen managed to keep afloat, but was unable to attract attention from any of the ships he saw. Then, the following night, he reported afterwards, he saw what appeared to be two shipmates walking across the water toward him. They told him, he said, that if he swam toward the moon he would reach safety. Nicolaysen did as they directed, and a few hours later he was picked up by the British tanker *British Surveyor*.

Mountain ghosts
Mountain climbers seem especially prone to seeing apparitions. Dr. Griffith Pugh, a British climber, noted more than 30 sightings of ghosts by fellow mountaineers. One American climber in the Himalayas claimed to have seen, only a few yards away, a familiar figure: the bartender of the fashionable 21 Club in New York City, a man who had died five years earlier. A British climber in the same mountains reported seeing the figures of two of his dead schoolmates. Both men were climbing without oxygen at a high altitude.

In these instances, the apparitions were of clearly recognizable people known to the witnesses. But there are other cases in which climbers have reported being accompanied by mysterious, unknown "companions," which appear to have no individual identity.

Comforting presences
During the unsuccessful British attempt of 1933 to reach the summit of Everest, Frank Smythe, climbing alone and without oxygen, felt that he was "accompanied by another," as he put it in his account of the expedition, *Camp Six* (1937). "This 'presence' was strong and friendly. In its company I could not feel lonely, neither could I come to any harm." This sensation was so vivid that, when Smythe paused for a moment to boost his strength with some mint cake, "instinctively I divided the mint into two halves and turned round with one half in my hand to offer it to my 'companion.'"

Others undergoing extreme physical stress, fatigue, and isolation, such as explorers and solo aviators, have

"Man" on the mountain
Named after the highest point in the Harz Mountains, Germany, this light diffraction phenomenon, known as the Brocken Bow, is often mistaken by mountaineers for the figure of a man.

HIGH RISK

Those climbing at high altitudes – anything over about 7,800 feet – are particularly prone to hallucinations, because there is less oxygen in the rarefied atmosphere. (The hallucinations may be accompanied by other symptoms, such as headache and nausea – a disorder known as altitude sickness.) In these conditions, oxygenation of the blood is reduced and an inadequate supply is carried to the brain, a condition known medically as cerebral hypoxemia. The brain then fails to function normally, and confusion, dizziness, poor coordination, and hallucinations may occur.

Cold and fatigue

Dr. Griffith Pugh reported the cases of two climbers in the Himalayas who saw visions of familiar figures when they had ascended to a height of 14,000 feet. In addition to the oxygen shortage at this height, they were experiencing extreme cold and fatigue – both of which can increase the risk of hallucinating.

provided similar accounts of being accompanied by various comforting presences. The British Antarctic explorer Sir Ernest Shackleton (1874–1922), describing a three-man trek across the mountains and glaciers of South Georgia island in 1915, wrote, in his account *South* (1919): "It often seemed to me that we were four, not three." And Frank Worsley, one of his companions on the expedition, recalling the journey in his memoirs, *Shackleton's Boat Journey* (1940), reflected: "Even now I again find myself counting our party – Shackleton, Crean, and I and – who was the other?"

In 1969 American pilot Edith Foltz-Stearns stated in an interview in the magazine *Fate*: "I never fly alone. Some 'presence' sits beside me, my 'co-pilot' ....In times of great danger some unseen hand actually takes the controls and guides me to safety."

Helpful companion

Foltz-Stearns's "companion," however, was not always the same person. In 1932, the aviator claimed, the voice that warned her not to make a dangerous landing was that of an old schoolmate who had died when still a girl. But, when she was ferrying a plane during the Second World War, the warning that saved her from flying into the side of a mountain came, she said, from her dead father.

> ## "I again find myself counting our party – Shackleton, Crean, and I and – who was the other?"

British publisher Peter Dawnay reported a presence similar to that noticed by Foltz-Stearns. In 1967 Dawnay had to drive across Spain, then take a ferry to Tunis, where he had an important appointment. His only hope of catching the ferry was to drive all night nonstop. During the taxing journey he sensed a presence in the seat beside him. This companion was invisible, but Dawnay remembers the feeling of reassurance it gave him.

Extreme stress can sometimes distort perceptions, and the apparitions seen in some of the cases just described may have been hallucinations. And in the cases of helpful or comforting presences, it is clear why such hallucinations would take that form.

Longing for help

When, for example, the sailor Arne Nicolaysen saw two crewmen approaching him across the water, he had been alone in the ocean for 24 hours with little prospect of rescue and was in a state of not only physical exhaustion but extreme fear and despair. He would have wished desperately that his shipmates could somehow rescue him, impossible though that might seem. In these circumstances, might not the apparitions he saw simply have been images conjured up by his subconscious mind to aid him in his hour of need?

Uncanny experience
Explorer Sir Ernest Shackleton, whose statue stands in Exhibition Road, London, sensed the presence of a mysterious companion throughout one expedition.

A TRIPLE HALLUCINATION?

On falling asleep or waking, a brother and his two sisters would see the baleful figure of their dead mother staring at them.

"*H*ER APPARITION COMES usually twice a week through the closed door of my bedroom and stops at the foot of the bed." — Mr. D. B.

"I have seen her, standing at my bed, just looking at me. Always I have tried to keep her out of my room, trying to push her away." — Miss J. B.

"She would come in, right through the panels in the door, and then would stop at my bed and gaze....I never told my brother and sister." — Mrs. V. B.

Sibling stress

This is a case of a brother and his two sisters claiming to have seen, independently of each other, the ghost of their recently dead mother. Yet what they saw may have been a collective hallucination, one induced by psychological stress. This is the theory advanced by a British physician, Dr. N. Lukianowicz, of Bristol, who reported the case in 1959 in the *Archives of General Psychiatry*. He termed it a hallucination à trois.

Mr. D. B. was a 30-year-old clerk at the time he reportedly began seeing the apparition in January 1957, shortly after his mother died. D. B. lived with his sister, Miss J. B., a 32-year-old stenographer, in the house they had inhabited with their mother.

In her last years, the mother had been chronically ill, suffering from stomach cancer and senile dementia. D. B. and J. B. nursed her at home, and their sister V. B., a 36-year-old married woman who lived on the same street, would often drop in to help.

Frightening experience

D. B. and his sisters reportedly saw their mother's figure most often while falling asleep or waking, a common time for visions. All three found the experience frightening: D. B. and V. B. reported that, upon seeing the apparition, they would hide under the bedclothes, and J. B. stated that she was sometimes too scared to move. D. B. and J. B. also apparently experienced auditory hallucinations. At breakfast they would often hear their mother's voice calling them from upstairs — but the brother always heard his name, the sister hers.

Three other sisters, who lived in another town, did not share the experiences of their siblings. Neither did V. B.'s husband: when she woke him on seeing the apparition in

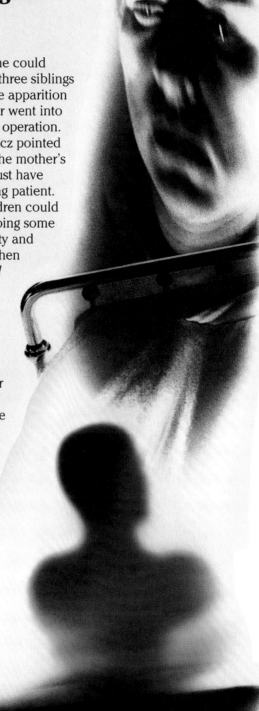

their bedroom, he could see nothing. All three siblings ceased to see the apparition when the brother went into a hospital for an operation.

Dr. Lukianowicz pointed out that during the mother's last years she must have been a very trying patient. "Hence her children could not help developing some repressed hostility and death wishes. When she died, *they all felt guilty* and responsible...."

The doctor later suggested that the three "were expecting a punishment for their matricidal wishes....Thus the image of their dead mother became...a real 'nightmare.'"

THE GHOST IN PERSPECTIVE

"Witness-related" ghosts, "place-related" ghosts, doppelgängers, out-of-body experiences, astral bodies, fantasies, time slips — numerous categories and explanations have been advanced to account for the variety of ghost experiences that have been reported.

OME GHOSTS SEEM DEFINITELY "witness-related" — they appear only to one or more particular individuals. The ghost of the mother in the Bristol triple haunting, for example, manifested itself only to the three children who had looked after her. If her other children had had the experience, it would have been far less meaningful — and if a stranger had seen the apparition, the incident would have been meaningless.

Often, as we have seen, the ghost appears not only to a particular individual but seemingly does so for a particular purpose — in many cases, to communicate a message, which is sometimes beneficial to the recipient. Whatever the exact nature of these witness-related ghosts — whether they are subjective or objective — their apparent purpose is to be seen by those who do see them and not by anyone else.

"Place-related"

If all ghosts were witness-related, it would simplify research into the enigma of ghosts. But many reported apparitions are of a distinctly different type: they are "place-related" — that is, they appear, not to a single particular person, but in a particular location to a variety of persons. The ghosts claimed to haunt a particular building, such as a castle or restaurant, are always confined to that building and are usually seen or sensed by an assortment of residents, staff, and visitors, who have little in common.

No message

Such ghosts have no particular significance for those who see them. They appear to have no message to communicate, no mission to fulfill. Descriptions of such specters show them apparently preoccupied with their own concerns — for example, looking sorrowful, wringing their hands, wailing, without any seeming interest in those who are observing them. Witnesses describe them as gliding from one place to another, apparently oblivious of the observer. In fact, the thought-provoking question arises: If it is assumed that these ghosts are objective phenomena, does it matter

> Some ghosts have no particular significance for those who see them. They appear to have no message to communicate, no mission to fulfill.

to them whether they are ever seen by anyone at all? These two basic types of ghost differ so much that they might seem to be quite separate entities. Yet they share a number of characteristics: both usually take the form of once-living people, both are insubstantial, and both are liable to vanish in a split second.

Seeing your own ghost

One particular type of reported apparition is the doppelgänger, a spectral double of yourself. In his book, *Hallucinations and Illusions* (1897), Edmund Parish relates an account of a doppelgänger experience told by a 39-year-old German mother: "One of the children was sleeping restlessly, I took the lamp to see if anything was wrong. As I drew back the curtain which shut off the bedroom, I saw two paces from me the image of myself stooping over the end of the bed, in a dress which I had not been wearing for some time: the figure was turned three-quarters away from me, the attitude expressed deep grief....I was neither specially sad nor specially excited that evening....

"Three months before I had lost one of my children. It has just occurred to me while writing this, that after death my child was laid across the foot of the bed, and I may have stood in that attitude then. The dress, too, was the one I was wearing at the time."

More than one self?

It is almost as if the mother had made a journey back in time to an earlier moment and was seeing the scene as if someone had made a video-recording of it. But generally, when we recall an incident from the past, we see it, as we lived through it before, subjectively. We do not see, as the German woman did, ourselves within the scene.

Double trouble
This illustration from Edgar Allan Poe's short story "William Wilson" shows the protagonist of the story after having stabbed his doppelgänger. He thereby ensured his own death.

Most researchers of psychic phenomena regard the doppelgänger as a kind of hallucination. But some suggest the highly theoretical possibility that we consist of more than one self, and that, in doppelgänger incidents, the self that is observing is a separate entity from the self that is being observed.

Floating in space

Another extraordinary phenomenon that has much in common with doppelgänger reports is the out-of-body experience (OBE). In this type of incident an individual has an impression of being detached from his or her physical body and floating in space. The experience is often reported by patients undergoing surgery under general anesthetic and some doctors have advanced the theory that it occurs just after clinical death. Indeed, some take such near-death experiences one step further, and claim that they provide persuasive evidence for the existence of an afterlife.

The usual theory advanced to explain OBE's is that they are illusions of some kind. But this does not explain how the

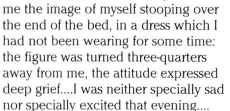

At times of extreme emotion or stress — such as terror, ecstasy, or awareness of impending death — the astral body is said to separate from the physical and move around outside it.

person reportedly having the experience can sometimes see what is happening elsewhere — in the corridor outside the operating theater, for example, or in a hospital ward — and, though apparently unconscious, may be able to hear what the doctors and nurses in the theater are saying. What this floating observer sees and hears is often found after the event to correspond in every detail with what actually took place at the time.

Such evidence suggests, however tentatively, that the individual's seat of awareness might have temporarily left the physical body, and thus was able to gather information.

Another body

A related possible explanation for such experiences is a highly speculative one — that we all consist of an astral as well as a physical body. This is an ancient concept, found in many cultures. According to this line of thinking, our astral body is normally completely coincident with the physical body (in some cultures it is believed that the astral body extends beyond the physical and that this is why we are sometimes aware of something near us even when it has not touched us). It is only, it is believed, at times of extreme emotion or stress — such as terror, ecstasy, or awareness of impending death — that the astral body is said to separate from the physical and move around outside it.

Brain irritation

Those who suffer from migraine headaches or epilepsy sometimes see lifelike images of themselves, a symptom known by the medical term of autoscopy. Neurologists believe that in these cases some form of irritation of the rear and side surfaces of the brain, produced by stress, may be responsible. This theory, suggesting a purely physical cause for such doppelgänger visions, may be correct. But, clearly, not everyone who suffers from migraine headaches or epilepsy experiences autoscopy.

Medical explanations, however, don't necessarily explain examples of the phenomenon that occur in unstressful

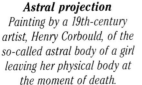

Astral projection
Painting by a 19th-century artist, Henry Corbould, of the so-called astral body of a girl leaving her physical body at the moment of death.

situations. In the April 1966 edition of *Fate* magazine, there is a story of a Boston man, John S., who saw his double. One day in 1962 he was sitting at home, perfectly relaxed, listening to a piece of classical orchestral music, when he looked up to see a duplicate of himself conducting the orchestra.

This vision, reminiscent of Oscar Levant's fantasy in the movie *An American in Paris* (1951), may similarly have been no more than fantasy. Perhaps the music had sent John S. into some form of reverie, in which his creative subconscious began playing tricks on his conscious mind.

Fantastic experiences

Some people are known to be more fantasy-prone than others. In psychological experiments conducted in the 1980's, for example, psychologists Sheryl Wilson and Theodore X. Barber, of Cushing Hospital, in Framingham, Massachusetts, found that about 1 person in 20 has a tendency to imagine taking part in fantastic experiences that are extremely vivid. And eminent psychical researchers Dr. Kenneth Ring and Dr. Christopher Rosing, at the University of Connecticut, have put forward the idea that some people are "encounter-prone" — that is, much more likely than others to imagine meeting ghosts or aliens.

Time slip?

Some accounts of seeing ghosts seem to involve what is known as a time slip. One striking case was recounted by Mrs. Elizabeth Denton, wife of a Boston professor of geology, in the book she wrote with her husband,

Psychical researcher
Dr. Kenneth Ring has suggested that some people are more likely to see what they think are ghosts, or, for example, extraterrestrial aliens, than others. His term to describe such people is "encounter-prone."

PET TELEPATHY?

Reports of people dreaming about their own deaths or the passing away of loved ones are standard fare in the annals of psychical literature. Not so common, however, are prophetic dreams of animal deaths.

The October 1904 edition of the *Journal* of the Society for Psychical Research contains a report submitted by the novelist Rider Haggard, author of *King Solomon's Mines* (1885). In the report, Haggard claimed that one morning he had a frightening dream: "A black retriever dog, a most amiable and intelligent beast named Bob, which was the property of my eldest daughter, was lying on its side among brushwood, or rough growth of some sort, by water....In my vision the dog was trying to speak to me in words, and failing, transmitted to my mind in an undefined fashion the knowledge that it was dying."

Hit by train

The dream proved prescient, because when a search was made later that day, the body of the dog was found: it had been hit by a train and was lying in a location roughly similar to that seen by Rider Haggard in his dream.

Author's vision
Rider Haggard claimed he had a dream which foretold the death of his daughter's dog.

The Soul of Things (1863). While traveling in the West in 1861, the Denton family was forced to wait a long time for a train at Joliet, Illinois. When it arrived, there was a 20-minute break for the passengers already on the train, who made their way to the station dining room. While her husband saw to the baggage, Mrs. Denton, accompanied by her children, selected a vacant car. She described what happened next: "Judge of my surprise, on glancing around, as I entered the car, to find it already crowded with passengers!...I was turning to find a vacant seat in another car, when a second glance around showed me that the passengers were rapidly losing their apparent entity, and in a moment they were to me invisible. I had had sufficient time to note the features, dress, and personal appearance of several, and, taking a seat, I awaited the return of the passengers....A number of those who returned to the car I recognised as being in every particular the counterparts of their late but transient representatives."

"Ethereal fluid"

Mrs. Denton went on to ask: "How could these individuals be seen in the car, when, in fact, they were not in the car at all, but in the dining room of the station? That the persons or images seen were indeed the individuals who at that moment were in

Mrs. Elizabeth Denton
This noted psychic and author wrote many accounts of her extrasensory experiences.

the station, I do not believe. That the persons who had so lately been sitting in the car...had radiated to the surrounding atmosphere that ethereal fluid which stamps upon it these images...I regard as a simple, safe, and natural conclusion."

In searching for a possible explanation for Mrs. Denton's unusual experience, if there is one, we need to bear in mind that she was a noted psychic (the book she co-authored is largely a chronicle of her extrasensory perceptions). During her long wait, she had been anxious whether her family would find seats, and this anxiety may have triggered her subconscious to create her vision.

True likenesses

Yet this does not explain how, if her story was accurate, she was able to see the true likenesses of passengers she had not yet encountered physically. Had their images persisted in the car in some immaterial form? Or had she somehow traveled back in time and seen the passengers as they were before they arrived at the station? Or did she imagine the whole thing, or perhaps make it up to further her career as a psychic?

We may occasionally think of time as a barrier that cannot be crossed. Yet in the case of ghosts, and those who reportedly have seen them, it may be that time is no barrier at all.

Ghost train?
An Illinois Central Railroad advertisement from the 1880's. On just such a train, the author, Mrs. Denton, saw apparitions of her fellow passengers.

ANIMAL GHOSTS

"I slammed the heavy door. Halfway across the gallery I looked back. The door was open again and a monstrous black cat crouched in the hall, its red-flecked amber eyes fixed on me."

THESE ARE THE WORDS OF IRISH ARTIST Tom McAssey, taken from an interview published in the *Dublin Evening Herald* in December 1968. The animal he described having seen, while painting in the gallery of the Dower House, Killakee, in the hills outside Dublin, is one of the most terrifying and best authenticated of animal ghosts, the Black Cat of Killakee. So convinced was McAssey that his vision was indeed that of the famous phantom beast that he immediately painted a likeness of it, and the portrait now hangs in the Killakee House restaurant.

Did McAssey indeed see an apparition of the cat, or was the sighting a figment of his artistic imagination? Over the past 200 years, others had reported seeing the specter — but this does not, of course, prove its existence.

Favorite dog
There are literally hundreds of published reports of animal ghosts. In many cases, the apparitions are of animals known to the witnesses. The case of Mrs. Mary Bagot, related in *Proceedings of the Society for Psychical Research* for 1898–99, lends some support to the view that animal ghosts do exist.

In March 1883, Mrs. Bagot and her daughter were on holiday at the Hôtel des Anglais in Menton, France. "I had left at home, in Norfolk," said Mrs. Bagot, "in the care of our gardener, a very favourite little dog, a black and tan terrier named Judy. I was sitting at dinner and suddenly saw my dog run across the room, and unthinkingly exclaimed, 'Why, there's Judy!'....A few days later I got a letter saying that Judy had been suddenly taken ill and died ....My impression is that she died the day I saw her."

Mrs. Bagot's story is supported by an entry in her daughter's journal. On March 24, 1883, she noted: "Mamma saw Judy's ghost at table d'hôte," then four days later she wrote: "Judy dead, poor dear."

In his *Annales des Sciences Psychiques* (1912), the French scientist and psychical investigator Camille Flammarion published the following account told him by a Swiss from Lausanne, Mr. M. G. Graeser: "I was a very solitary boy, preferring study to socialising: my one companion was my Saint Bernard, Boby, who was with me constantly. On December 14,

> "A few days later I got a letter saying that Judy had been suddenly taken ill and died.... My impression is that she died the day I saw her."

1910, Boby was with my parents in Lausanne, two kilometres away. About 7:30 P.M. I heard the door of my room open and saw Boby standing in the doorway, looking unhappy. I called him to me: he didn't look up and he didn't obey my order. I called again, he came, rubbed against my legs, and lay down on the floor at my feet. I bent to stroke him — and he wasn't there!" Some strange intuition made Graeser rush to the telephone and call the veterinarian, who informed him that Boby had been put to sleep some two minutes earlier.

Distress signal
If these stories have any validity, it may be possible that an animal, on the point of or close to death, emits a kind of distress signal, which is picked up by a person attached to the animal. In the same way that human apparitions reportedly materialize to loved ones when they are about to die, so might favorite pets seem to appear fleetingly to say their farewells.

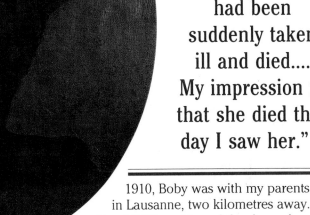

The Black Cat of Killakee
Tom McAssey's portrait of this monstrous phantom cat was painted shortly after he allegedly saw the apparition.

FACT OR FIGMENT?

Ghosts seen by more than one person, exorcisms, and crisis apparitions are all cited by some as evidence of the objective reality of ghosts. But is such evidence as convincing as it at first appears?

"IT WAS IN ZURICH, October 18, 1940. I took my usual way back to work after lunch; it was 1:45 P.M. As I walked along towards the Obere Zaeune, I suddenly saw my father. Strange, I thought, he's been away for the last fortnight, why has he come back so unexpectedly? I hastened my steps and called out: 'Hello father!' The words were hardly out of my mouth when he disappeared."

Mr. F., the Swiss who had this experience — recorded by German psychologist Aniela Jaffé in her book _Apparitions and Precognition_ (1963) — said he was "deeply perplexed" by the encounter. And when later that day he received a phone call telling him his father

"Our father, who had loved us so much, had wanted to show himself to us once more as he was when still alive. It was his farewell."

had died the previous night, he was even more upset and emotionally distraught. He immediately phoned his sister to give her the bad news and share with her his eerie experience. "What did she tell me?" he asked in astonishment. "I could hardly believe my ears. At that very time, father had appeared to her in the Bahnhof-strasse, and had suddenly disappeared again."

Cases such as these, where the same ghost is allegedly seen by more than one person, and where no psychological stress seems to be involved, present a challenge to those who are skeptical about the existence of ghosts. Yet many would simply accept Mr. F.'s own explanation: "Our father, who had loved us so much, had wanted to show himself to us once more as he was when still alive. It was his farewell."

Evil spirits

Multiple-witness sightings of the kind claimed by Mr. F. are not the only experiences that support the argument that ghosts exist as objective entities. Another factor that might appear to strengthen this argument is exorcism. Since ancient times, exorcism has been practiced to cast out evil spirits from a possessed body or property — in many cases with reported success.

Such successes seem to provide some evidence that these types of spirits might exist. Yet how important is

this evidence? Those who have absolute belief in a faith healer, for example, can apparently be helped with their physical ills. In much the same way, might not those who believe in exorcism be purged of certain psychological ills, or "inner demons," as the exorcist would choose to term them?

There are many reports of people turning to exorcism as a last resort — and being surprised by the results. Usually these are cases involving an apparently objective ghost — that is, a haunting spirit seen independently by more than one witness.

The exorcist
Canon Pearce-Higgins, one-time vice-provost of Southwark cathedral in London, claimed to have exorcised many ghosts.

Ghost soother
The late Canon John Pearce-Higgins, at one time vice-chairman of the Church of England's Fellowship for Psychical Study, claimed that he had "cleared up" many houses during his ministry as vice-provost of Southwark cathedral, in southeast London.

One ghost that the canon says he "soothed and persuaded to go away" was that of a man who used to live in Lewisham, a suburb of London. About 20 years ago two brothers claimed that they had been repeatedly disturbed by an apparition whose habit it was to stamp loudly up and down the stairs during the night. Terrified by these seemingly supernatural noises, the brothers eventually turned to the church for help.

Apparent success
The canon claimed that he discovered the alleged ghost to be that of a man who had occupied the second-floor apartment in the house for many years. After the death of this man's wife, the brothers had persuaded him, perhaps rather forcibly, to move down to the

basement. "After he died, he evidently returned to show his disapproval!" Canon Pearce-Higgins told the author and psychical investigator Peter Underwood, who later recorded the case in his book *Exorcism!* (1990). "I persuaded him that he had had his revenge and he could go away — and he went....I believe as a Christian that it is the Church's job to tell earthbound spirits to go on and up and not to hang around down here," the canon concluded.

> "I believe as a Christian that it is the Church's job to tell earthbound spirits to go on and up and not to hang around down here."

If Canon Pearce-Higgins was successful, as he claimed, this does not necessarily present categorical evidence for the existence of ghosts. The supernatural noises the brothers said they had heard may have been what are known to researchers of the paranormal as auditory hallucinations, and it may have been simply some sort of termination of these that the canon achieved. Or it may have been that the brothers invented the whole story of the haunting — and its cessation.

Spirit messages
Even reportedly successful exorcisms, therefore, do not furnish the skeptic with incontrovertible proof that ghosts are real. Another, perhaps stronger, kind of evidence for the reality of ghosts may be provided by crisis apparitions.

One such case was recounted by Elliott O'Donnell in his book *Ghosts Helpful and Harmful* (1924). Some time in the early 1920's, Mr. K. of Bristol, England, was sitting in his study one afternoon, when he fell, or thought he fell, asleep. He dreamed that he woke up with a start, to see the door opening very slowly to reveal his friend B. entering the room on tiptoe. Putting a finger to his lips, as if to request silence, B. then took out a razor, bared the blade, and made as if to cut his own throat.

K. immediately realized B.'s intention, and a furious struggle ensued between the two men. The result was that both fell to the floor with a resounding crash and K. woke up with a start. Because the dream had seemed so vivid and real to

FAKE EXORCISM

A newlywed woman was convinced she was possessed by evil spirits. A Christian healer practiced a fake exorcism — and she was cured....

SOME BELIEVE THAT THE SUCCESS of many alleged exorcisms can be attributed to psychological factors rather than physical ones. They argue that so-called possession by evil spirits lies in the mind of the sufferer and that, when an exorcist attempts to banish a spirit, all he is in fact doing is banishing the *idea* of the spirit. As long as the sufferer has absolute faith in the exorcist's powers, he or she will then feel freed from the alleged possession.

Supposed sham

In his book on demoniac possession, *Le Diable et la Possession Démoniaque* (1975), the French writer Hervé Masson relates the story of a supposedly sham exorcism that took place on the island of Mauritius in 1947. A newlywed woman called Farida was very sick, afflicted with the idea that she had been possessed by evil spirits. The healers and magicians of her native religion were unable to cure her, so she turned in despair to a Christian healer for help.

Healer's "negotiations"

Initially, this healer was reluctant to intervene: he simply did not believe in the demons' existence. But after meeting Farida, he agreed to try to help her. Masson claims that the healer "negotiated" with the demons within Farida, persuading them that if they continued to possess her, they would destroy her, thus rendering themselves homeless. The healer told them that it was in their own interests to find a more suitable residence. Apparently, the exorcism was successful: Farida recovered.

Complete charade

The entire exorcism was, in fact, a charade. Masson says that the healer had realized that he could not effect a "cure" unless he dealt with the situation on Farida's terms. He pretended to believe in the demons, in order to gain Farida's confidence. Once this was achieved, he was able to convince her that he was in dialogue with the demons and that they had agreed to his requests to leave her body.

This story seems to suggest that many exorcisms might be of the same nature as the "banishment" of Farida's "evil spirits" — that is, no more than a form of psychotherapy.

him, K. had difficulty reconciling himself to the fact that that was all it was — simply a dream. His perplexity increased when he looked to see what time it was, and noted that the glass of his watch had mysteriously broken.

The following day he bumped into B. and was astonished to note how pale and drawn he looked. B. immediately related the following story: "Things haven't gone too well with me lately, and yesterday afternoon I determined to put an end to myself by cutting my throat. I had got my razor, all ready to do the deed, when what I took to be you — if it wasn't you it was certainly your double — came running in at my door and caught hold of me by the wrist. We had a terrible tussle and in the end fell on the ground. No sooner had we crashed against the boards than you vanished."

Distress signal

If K. and B. were telling the truth, perhaps some form of extrasensory perception (ESP) was involved — with K.'s subconscious mind picking up on a kind of distress signal sent out by B. But to hypothesize about ESP is to try to explain one unknown with another. Alternatively, some might argue that B. had a guardian angel in the spirit world, that of either some deceased relative or friend, one that communicated with K. and sent him (in apparition form) to the rescue. Skeptics, certainly, might dismiss the case as one of purely coincidental hallucinations.

Convincing visions

Some ghosts have been seen in such clear and vivid detail that this is sometimes regarded as an argument for their objective existence. Yet it doesn't have to be. The same lifelike distinctness is a characteristic of some visions known to be hallucinations. A well-documented case of a man to whom this applied was published in

1904 in *Proceedings* of the British Society for Psychical Research. Mr. A., who had lost the sight of his left eye and had a defective right eye, constantly hallucinated. Sometimes his visions were of banal images, such as a wall beside the road; at other times, they were almost psychedelic, with coiling serpents and brightly colored flowers depicted in detail. Whatever Mr. A. saw was, interestingly, notable for its distinctness; in fact, the hallucinations were far clearer than anything he could see with his defective eyesight.

Sunlit dress

One day Mr. A. was walking with a friend to the railway station when he "saw" a woman ahead. According to the narrator of the account, John Honeyman, "What Mr. A. saw as distinctly as anything he had ever seen in his life was the figure of a female walking closely in front of him, so that he could hardly step without treading on her skirt. The dress (which he was able to describe in the minutest detail) was beautifully illuminated with sunlight and moved naturally in response to the motion of the figure, while the

> It is evident, however, that if Mr. A. had not been so aware of his tendency to hallucinate, he might well have believed his visions were ghosts.

light silk jacket was occasionally lifted as if by the breeze. Mr. A. made a motion of putting the skirt out of his way with his umbrella, but of course, as he knew, there was nothing there."

The reasons for Mr. A. hallucinating in the way he did were never established — whether the vivid images he saw were neurologically linked to his defective vision or had no connection with it. It is evident, however, that if Mr. A. had not been so aware of his tendency to hallucinate, he might well have believed his visions were ghosts.

Guardian angel
This 19th-century painting by an anonymous German artist portrays a child protected by her guardian angel. In Christianity, Judaism, and Islam, such spirits are believed to protect and guide not only individuals but nations. In cases where a person about to commit suicide is allegedly prevented from doing so by the apparition of a relative or friend, some believe that the latter has received a message from the would-be suicide's guardian angel.

THE NATURE OF THE GHOST

Some ghosts seem to exist only in the mind, others seem to have an objective reality, while others seem to be created by some form of collaboration between the seer and the seen.

THE APPARENT contributions made to each ghost-seeing experience by the seer (witness) and the seen (agent) vary in their proportions from one incident to another — but these experiences can be broken down into three basic types.

◆ *First type: the witness seems to be entirely responsible for the apparition.* Doppelgängers and what are thought to be hallucinations appear to fall into this category. Sightings of animal ghosts would also have to be included (as hallucinations) in this class — at least, for those who assume that animals do not continue to exist after their death and, this being so, are unable to project their plight into the consciousness of human beings.

◆ *Second type: the agent seems to be predominantly responsible.* Most of the apparitions reportedly seen in haunted places belong to this type. Whether these apparitions are considered to be revenants (a French word for spirits which return after death), astral bodies, or earthbound spirits, there are grounds for believing that they may be entities with some kind of objective reality. But even if they are, it is evident that only certain people can see them. It may be that these are persons with marked psychic abilities; or they may be people not usually especially psychic who are, at the time of the sighting, in a state of particularly heightened awareness.

◆ *Third type: there seems to be some form of collaboration between witness and agent.* This theory, advanced by Hilary Evans, the British writer on the

> **Despite all our exercises in analysis and categorizing, the mysteries that remain are far greater than any explanations that might shed light on the subject.**

paranormal, appears to apply particularly to the classic "crisis apparition" case. In this, all the evidence indicates that it is impossible, by normal means, for the witness to know of the agent's crisis and equally impossible for the agent to know of the witness's location and circumstances in order to impart information about the crisis to him or her. If this is so, how does the crisis apparition occur? Evans suggests that the psyches of witness and agent might meet and create the ghost-seeing experience between them — although he is the first to admit that how this would happen is beyond the realm of present understanding.

Profound mysteries

In the end, however, despite all our exercises in analysis and categorizing, the mysteries that remain are far greater than any explanations that might shed light on the subject. If ghosts do exist objectively, what, as visible entities, do they consist of? Is their essence compatible with the natural physical laws that account for and govern light, radio waves, X-rays, and other such phenomena — or does it lie beyond them? If ghosts are truly the spirits of dead people, why, to repeat the question we asked at the beginning of this chapter, do so very few show themselves? And why are ghost sightings so uncommon?

It may be that these are mysteries too deep for human beings ever to fathom. But psychical researchers will continue to investigate ghost sightings, and man will never cease to ponder the question: Do ghosts exist?

INDEX

Page numbers in **bold** type refer to illustrations and captions.

PHOTOGRAPHIC SOURCES